A Teacher's Guide to

Mentor Texts

Grades K–5

A Teacher's Guide to

Mentor Texts

grades K-5

Carl Anderson

Heinemann
Portsmouth, NH

Heinemann
145 Maplewood Avenue, Suite 300
Portsmouth, NH 03801
www.heinemann.com

"Dedicated to Teachers" is a trademark of Greenwood Publishing Group, LLC

The author and publisher wish to thank those who have generously given permission to reprint borrowed material:

"What do we mean by . . ." tweet by @FletcherRalph on February 18, 2022. Reprinted by permission Ralph Fletcher.

"Students need to read as . . ." tweet by @Tom_Newkirk on December 5, 2021. Reprinted by permission of Tom Newkirk.

Excerpts from *Finding the Heart of Nonfiction: Teaching 7 Essential Craft Tools with Mentor Texts* by Georgia Heard. Copyright © 2013 by Georgia Heard. Published by Heinemann, Portsmouth, NH. Reprinted by permission of the publisher. All rights reserved.

JABARI JUMPS. Copyright © 2017 by Gaia Cornwall. Reproduced by permission of the publisher, Candlewick Press, Somerville, MA.

"Surprising Saturn" by Liz Huyck, *Ask*, November 2019 © by Cricket Media, Inc. Reproduced with permission. All Cricket Media material is copyrighted by Cricket Media and/or various authors and illustrators.

Any commercial use or distribution of material without permission is strictly prohibited. Please visit https://cricketmedia.com/childrens-content-licensingfor licensing and http://www.cricketmedia.com for subscriptions.

"Summer Homework Should Be Banned" by Nancy Kalish. From *TIME for Kids.* © 2009 TIME USA LLC. All rights reserved. Used under license.

p. 60, online resources: 6–7 NASA/JPL/Space Science Institute; p. 61, online resources: 6–7 NASA/JPL/Space Science Institute; 7 (RB) NASA/JPL–Caltech; 7 (RT) ©Peter Hermes Furian/Shutterstock; 7 (RT-2) © Macrovector/Shutterstock; p. 63, online resources: 8 (BC) NASA/JPL–Caltech/SSI; 8 (LT) NASA/JPL–Caltech; 8 (RB) NASA/JPL–Caltech/Space Science Institute/Hampton University; 8 (RC) NASA/JPL–Caltech/SSI/Cornell; 8 (RT-2) © Imfoto/Shutterstock; 8–11 © M. Aurelius/Shutterstock; 10 (LB) NASA/JPL–Caltech/Space Science Institute; 10 (LT) NASA/JPL–Caltech/Space Science Institute; 10 (RB) NASA, ESA, JPL, SSI, and Cassini Imaging Team; 10 (RT) NASA/JPL–Caltech/Space Science Institute; online resources: 8–11 © M. Aurelius/Shutterstock; 9 (LB) NASA/JPL–Caltech/Space Science Institute; 9 (RB) NASA/JPL–Caltech/Space Science Institute/Hampton University; 11 (BC) NASA/JPL–Caltech.

credits continue on page 127

Library of Congress Control Number: 2022941884
978-0-325-13281-5

Editor: Heather Anderson
Production: Patty Adams
Cover and interior designs: Vita Lane
Videography: Paul Tomasyan, Dennis Doyle, and Sherry Day
Typesetting: Vita Lane and Gina Poirier Design
Manufacturing: Val Cooper

Printed in the United States of America on acid-free paper
2 3 4 5 MP 26 25 24 23   PO#4500870768

For Katie Wood Ray—
look what you started!

Book Map

Online Resources

How to Access the Online Resources and Videos

To access the Online Resources for *A Teacher's Guide to Mentor Texts, Grades K–5*:

1. Go to **http://hein.pub/MentorK-5-login**.

2. Log in with your username and password. If you do not already have an account with Heinemann, you will need to create an account.

3. On the Welcome page, choose "Click here to register an Online Resource."

4. Register your product by entering the code **MENTORK-5** (be sure to read and check the acknowledgment box under the keycode).

5. Once you have registered your product, it will appear alphabetically in your account list of My Online Resources.

Note: When returning to Heinemann.com to access your previously registered products, simply log into your Heinemann account and click on "View my registered Online Resources."

About the Online Resources and Videos in This Book

The online resources for _A Teacher's Guide to Mentor Texts K-5_ include student writing and mentor texts that are discussed in the book, as well as forms, charts, and table tents that will help you as you teach with mentor texts.

Online Resource 1.1	Student Writing: Danya's "Goofy Gorilla" book
Online Resource 1.2	Student Writing: Alyssa's "Skateboarding! For beginners"
Online Resource 3.1	Mentor Text Planning Form
Online Resource 4.1	Link to "Surprising Saturn"
Online Resource 4.2	Link to "Summer Homework Should Be Banned"
Online Resource 4.3	Guide to Analyzing a Mentor Text
Online Resource 5.1	Table Tent: Whole-Class Immersion
Online Resource 5.2	Blank Form: Small-Group Immersion: Responding as Readers
Online Resource 5.3	Blank Form: Small-Group Immersion: Responding as Writers
Online Resource 6.1	Blank Version of Whole-Class Text Study Chart
Online Resource 6.2	Table Tent: Whole-Class Text Study
Online Resource 7.1	Table Tent: Mini-Lesson (Direct Instruction)
Online Resource 7.2	Table Tent: Mini-Lesson (Inquiry)
Online Resource 7.3	Table Tent: Small-Group Lesson (Direct Instruction)
Online Resource 7.4	Table Tent: Small-Group Lesson (Inquiry)
Online Resource 7.5	Table Tent: Writing Conference (Direct Instruction)
Online Resource 7.6	Table Tent: Writing Conference (Inquiry)
Online Resource 7.7	10 Tips for Conferring with Student Writers Online

You'll also find a welcome video, and 23 videos of Carl teaching that will help you envision the work you're reading about at various points in the book. Along with these videos, you'll find commentary from Carl that will help you better understand the teaching you see.

Video 1.1	Welcome Reader
Video 5.1	Immersion with Primary Students
Video 5.2	Immersion with Upper-Grade Students
Video 6.1	Whole-Class Text Study with Primary Students
Video 6.2	Whole-Class Text Study with Upper-Grade Students
Video 7.1	Direct Instruction Mini-lesson–Primary Grades
Video 7.2	Inquiry Mini-lesson–Primary Grades
Video 7.3	Direct Instruction Mini-lesson–Upper Grades
Video 7.4	Inquiry Mini-lesson–Upper Grades
Video 7.5	Small-Group Lesson–Primary Grades
Video 7.6	Small-Group Lesson–Upper Grades
Videos 7.7–7.13	Writing Conferences–Primary Grades
Videos 7.14–7.19	Writing Conferences–Upper Grades

What is a Mentor Text?

In Beverly Cleary's book *Ramona Quimby, Age 8,* Ramona's teacher, Mrs. Whaley, assigns her class a book report. She tells her students she wants them to "sell the book" to their classmates.

Ramona is anxious about the assignment. She wants her report about her book, *Left-Behind Cat*, to be interesting, unlike the boring ones that her sister Beezus says kids write that end with platitudes like "If you want to know what happens next, read the book."

To help sell her book, Ramona uses what she learns from watching . . . a cat food commercial! As she writes her report, Ramona incorporates what she noticed about how the writers of the commercial gave it rhythm and cadence to get viewers to take notice and, hopefully, buy their product:

> **Kids who have tried *Left-Behind Cat* are all smiles, smiles, smiles. *Left-Behind Cat* is the book kids ask for by name. Kids can read it every day and thrive on it. The happiest kids read *Left-Behind Cat* . . .**

For decades, readers have loved reading about the ever-resourceful Ramona who, in this story, reads a *mentor text* like a writer to help her figure out how to craft her writing. How can you help your students be like Ramona?

The answer is to put mentor texts at the center of how you teach writing. By doing so, you'll be able to show your students how to learn from them like Ramona does. When you use mentor texts to teach writing, you're doing one of the most important things you can to help students learn to write well.

A mentor text is a well-written text you show students to help them see how they can craft their own writing and also how to use writing conventions effectively. Mentor texts can be published texts by well-known authors, texts you've written yourself, or texts written by your students.

The word *mentor* is a reference to the ancient Greek epic poem, *The Odyssey* (Heard 2013; Panagiotakopoulos 2019). You may remember from your high school English class that when Odysseus left home for the Trojan War, he left his son Telemachus in the care of a guardian named Mentor. Later in the story, the goddess Athena disguised herself as Mentor and gave Telemachus advice on how to deal with his personal dilemmas. Just like Telemachus learned from Mentor/Athena, your students will learn about writing from the authors of mentor texts. And although you won't have to disguise yourself as a Greek god, you'll similarly guide students as they learn from these texts.

▷ **Video 1.1** *Welcome Reader*

• WORDS FROM TEACHING MENTORS •

> *"Mentor texts enable student writers to become connected to the dynamic world of professional writers."*
>
> **Allison Marchetti and Rebekah O'Dell (2015)**

• WORDS FROM A TEACHING MENTOR •

> *"Mentor texts are words that writers wish they had written themselves."*
>
> **Georgia Heard (2013)**

What Is a Mentor Text?

Q & A

What do we mean by *craft* and *conventions*?

When we write, we have to decide *what* a piece will be about. And we have to decide *how* we are going to write the piece. When we talk about the craft of writing and writing conventions, we're talking about *how* a piece is written.

Experienced writers know a great deal about the craft of writing. When they write a text, they draw upon their knowledge of the ways introductions and endings can go, the kinds of transitions writers use to move readers from part to part, the types of details they can include in a section, the ways sentences can be structured, and much more.

The terms *craft technique, crafting technique*, and *craft move* are synonyms that refer to the specific aspects of craft writers decide to use in a piece of writing. For example, when writers decide to start a nonfiction piece with a question lead, they are using a craft technique, as is the decision to begin a narrative scene with a time transition. Likewise, when writers decide to use various types of detail, such as dialogue and character actions and feelings, they're using crafting techniques. And when writers write a list of adjectives, they are making a craft move.

Experienced writers also know a great deal about writing *conventions*, the commonly accepted ways to make texts clear and understandable to readers. Conventions include punctuation, capitalization, grammar, and paragraphing.

When writers write well—that is, they use crafting techniques and conventions successfully—we say their writing has the *qualities of good writing* (focus, structure, detail, voice, and conventions). For example, when a writer includes action and descriptive facts in their nonfiction writing, we say their writing is *detailed*. Or when a writer skillfully uses the craft moves of speaking directly to the reader, or writing bold or italicized words, we say that their writing has *voice*.

It's important to note the illustrations in texts are crafted, and illustrators make numerous craft moves, too. For example, illustrators use the craft technique of zooming in to their subject (as well as zooming out to show an entire scene). And they use the crafting technique of motion lines to indicate movement.

Over the course of the year, you will use mentor texts to teach lessons about every quality of writing. Some of these lessons include:

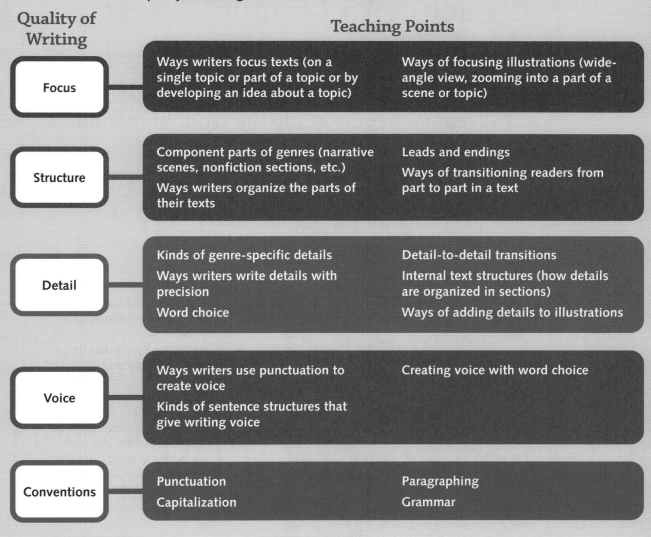

Quality of Writing

Teaching Points

Focus
- Ways writers focus texts (on a single topic or part of a topic or by developing an idea about a topic)
- Ways of focusing illustrations (wide-angle view, zooming into a part of a scene or topic)

Structure
- Component parts of genres (narrative scenes, nonfiction sections, etc.)
- Ways writers organize the parts of their texts
- Leads and endings
- Ways of transitioning readers from part to part in a text

Detail
- Kinds of genre-specific details
- Ways writers write details with precision
- Word choice
- Detail-to-detail transitions
- Internal text structures (how details are organized in sections)
- Ways of adding details to illustrations

Voice
- Ways writers use punctuation to create voice
- Kinds of sentence structures that give writing voice
- Creating voice with word choice

Conventions
- Punctuation
- Capitalization
- Paragraphing
- Grammar

Why Is It So Important to Teach with Mentor Texts?

When you use mentor texts in these ways, you are doing big work that will help your students grow as writers. Here's why.

1. Creative people study the work of mentors.

When you read about creative people, such as designers, painters, and musicians, you'll find they learn how to craft their work from studying the work of exemplary people in their fields and others that inspire them:

Maya Lin, the designer of the Vietnam Memorial in Washington, DC, was influenced by East Asian design ideas such as simplicity and sensitivity to landscape, as well as by studying the Memorial Rotunda at Yale University, where she was a student when she came up with her design for the Vietnam Memorial (Klein 2020; Park 2020).

Painter Jacob Lawrence, whose many works include *The Migration Series*, a group of sixty paintings that depict the Great Migration of Black Americans from the South to the North in the first part of the twentieth century, studied the paintings of Mexican muralist José Clemente Orozco. Lawrence incorporated what he learned about structure and color from Orozco into his own work (The Whitney Museum 2020–21).

When the rock group The Beatles went into the studio to record new songs, they often played songs by their favorite musicians, such as Chuck Berry, Little Richard, and Buddy Holly, and then used some of the musical "moves" they heard in these songs in their own compositions (Jackson 2021).

What Is a Mentor Text?

→ Recently, educators have written about combining writing and reading workshop into what they call *literacy studio* (Keene 2022) or *literacy workshop* (Walther and Biggs-Tucker 2020). In these models, students can readily see the connections between writing and reading.

2. Students learn that writing and reading are interconnected.

When you read profiles of authors, you'll find they read the writing of other writers and learn from them ways to write their own texts, just like other kinds of creative people do when they study the work of their mentors. There is a special term that we use for this kind of reading—*reading like a writer*.

Students often consider writing and reading to be separate subjects in school, which makes sense considering they often have writing and reading workshops scheduled at different times each day. When you teach with mentor texts and help students learn to read like writers, you are showing them that writing and reading are not separate activities, but are actually linked closely together. Realizing that they'll become better writers by doing a lot of reading is one of the most important insights that your students will learn in your writing workshop!

• **WORDS FROM A TEACHING MENTOR** •

"Not all readers are writers, but all writers are readers."

Ralph Fletcher (2013)

A Teacher's Guide to Mentor Texts

3. Mentor texts help students navigate each stage of the writing process.

As students move through the stages of the writing process—rehearsal, drafting, revising, editing, and publishing—what they learn from reading mentor texts helps them navigate each stage:

Rehearsal

As part of the *rehearsal* stage of the writing process, writers envision how a draft will go before they start to write it, often by touching each page of a book before they start drafting, or by making a flowchart, web, or outline. To do this work well, writers think about mentor texts they've read and what they've noticed about the way the authors organized them, and then writers use what they've learned to help them structure their own writing.

Drafting

When writers are in the *drafting* stage of the writing process, they envision each part of the draft before they write it—how they'll write the lead, what kind of details they'll use to compose each section, which punctuation marks they'll use to give sentences cadence and voice, how they'll end the text. As they make these decisions during the drafting process, writers think about how the authors of the mentor texts they've read use these craft techniques, and then they try them out in their drafts.

Revising

Next writers *revise*, or make changes to their draft to make it a better piece of writing. There are hundreds of kinds of revisions that writers make, from reworking a lead, reorganizing the sections, adding detail to a section, or shortening a sentence. One way writers decide what changes to make is by comparing what they've done to what they've seen other writers do in mentor texts that they've read.

Editing

Once revisions are complete, writers *edit* their writing for errors. They bring to the editing process a visual memory of how sentences are written and punctuated in the mentor texts they've read.

Publishing

Finally, writers *publish* their writing, that is, make it public by sharing it with readers. Today, the publishing process often involves making decisions about layout and graphics, decisions that writers are able to make with more panache if they've seen how other writers and illustrators made these decisions in similar texts.

4. Mentor texts enable you to teach writing descriptively.

Students aren't the only ones who benefit from mentor texts—you'll also benefit as a teacher from using them in your writing workshop.

One of the challenges you face in your teaching is figuring out how to explain with precision something that writers do in texts. When you use mentor texts in your teaching, you have concrete examples at your fingertips. You can describe them for your students in mini-lessons, small groups, and writing conferences. This is enormously helpful for students, as they both *see* the example from a mentor text and *hear* you describe what the writer has done.

Using mentor texts to explain with precision how writers craft their texts is a very different approach to teaching writing. Traditionally, teachers have taught writing *prescriptively*. That is, they have told students what to do when they write in ways that are too general to be of use to students.

Here are a few things teachers typically say about writing to students. Contrast these with the excerpts from texts that show what writers actually do when they craft their writing—and with how you could describe with precision what writers actually do when they compose texts:

• WORDS FROM A TEACHING MENTOR •

"What do we mean by craft in writing? I think of the writer's craft as the intentional use of language to create the effect you want. All writers must decide WHAT to write about, but that's just the first step. Craft involves HOW you write about your subject."

Ralph Fletcher (2022)

Instead of prescriptively telling students what to do as writers . . .	Show them a mentor text . . .	That will allow you to describe precisely what writers do.
"Write an introduction that hooks your readers."	"Evelyn Del Rey is my mejor amiga, my número uno best friend." (From *Evelyn Del Rey Is Moving Away*, by Meg Medina)	"There are lots of ways to begin stories, and Meg Medina uses a really powerful one in *Evelyn Del Rey Is Moving Away*. She starts by giving readers an important background detail—that Evelyn is the best friend of the narrator, Daniela. By revealing this detail at the very beginning of the story, Meg Medina helps us understand immediately how big a deal it is that Evelyn is moving away."
"Add lots of detail to your writing."	"Lurking below the water's surface, a croc lies in wait for its prey. When an unsuspecting animal passes by, the 1,000-pound beast explodes out of the water, grabs its victim, and drags it under the water to drown. Yikes!" (From *Deadliest Animals*, by Melissa Stewart)	"In this section, Melissa Stewart elaborates by writing several action facts—in this case, things that crocodiles do with their bodies. We learn what crocodiles do with their whole bodies—'the 1,000-pound beast explodes out of the water'—and also a part of its body, its claws—'grabs its victim' and 'drags it under the water to drown.'"

5. Mentor texts help students teach themselves about writing.

It's important you realize that no matter how good a writing teacher you are, you can't possibly teach your students everything they need to become good writers. There is just too much to learn about writing and not enough time for you to teach all of it, either in a unit of study, across a school year, or even during many years of writing instruction. Writes educator Frank Smith (1983), "[W]riting requires an enormous fund of specialized knowledge which cannot be acquired from lectures, textbooks, drill, trial and error, or even from the exercise of writing itself."

How, then, will students manage to learn all they need to become good writers? Or continue to learn about writing even after they leave your writing workshop? The answer is to surround them with mentor texts!

Just by hearing mentor texts read aloud, reading mentor texts to themselves, and looking at mentor texts that you project via a document camera or SMART Board, your students will learn about aspects of writing you haven't explicitly taught, as they continually read texts like a writer.

And, with your guidance, students will get better at reading like a writer during the time they spend in your writing workshop. They'll bring their improved ability to read like a writer into the future and will continue to learn about writing, even when they're not in a writing workshop—by finding and studying their own mentor texts.

What Is a Mentor Text?

You Can Teach with Mentor Texts in Many Ways:

You'll teach with mentor texts in writing workshop, when students are composing pieces of writing, and with instruction from you, are becoming better writers. Each day of writing workshop is part of a multi-week unit of study, during which you'll teach your class about an aspect of craft or process.

Mini-lesson (10–12 minutes)

A mini-lesson is a whole-class lesson about a writing strategy, craft technique, or language convention. When mini-lessons focus on craft or conventions, you'll teach with mentor texts.

Independent writing (25–30 minutes)

Students work on their writing. As students write, you'll have 1:1 writing conferences with several of them, and also lead small-group lessons. When conferences and small-group lessons are about craft or conventions, you'll teach with mentor texts.

Share session (5–10 minutes)

The class reconvenes to discuss how writing went that day, either to highlight student work, or to give feedback to a few students about their drafts-in-process.

On some days of units, you'll suspend the usual stucture of writing workshop:

Immersion

During the first few days of a craft unit of study, you'll *immerse* your students in the mentor texts you'll be teaching within the unit. You'll do this by reading the texts aloud, and by having students read some of them themselves.

Whole-class text study

Also in craft studies, you'll devote one or several days to *whole-class text study*, in which you'll guide your class as they study mentor texts from the current unit, and discuss with their classmates what they notice about them.

There are several books that give an overview of writing workshop: Katherine Bomer and Corrine Aren's *A Teacher's Guide to Writing Workshop Essentials* (2020), Ralph Fletcher and JoAnn Portalupi's *Writing Workshop: The Essential Guide* (2001b), and Stacey Shubitz and Lynne Dorfman's *Welcome to Writing Workshop* (2019).

• WORDS FROM A TEACHING MENTOR •

"I can't help students write well by myself. I need lots of help doing this teaching work, and I have found that help on the shelves of my library."

Katie Wood Ray, 1999

Examples of How Mentor Texts Help Children Write Well

Consider two students who wrote "under the influence" of mentor texts their teachers shared with their classes. As you read their writing, you'll see they used many crafting techniques and writing conventions they learned about from reading and studying these mentor texts in writing workshop:

Danya's Book, Grade 1

On the cover, Danya zooms in on the face of the gorilla who is the subject of her story. She also uses alliteration in her title.

Danya fills the entire page with the illustration of the scene, and embeds the text within the illustration. She also includes "talk bubbles" in the illustration

Suddenly one of the gorillas started to poop! I was so surprised. My mouth fell open.

Danya tells her emotional response and writes an action that shows this feeling. She begins sentences with capital letters and ends them with periods and exclamation marks.

Danya includes a secondary story in the illustration—her sister's inability to see what is happening with the gorilla—and dramatizes it with talk bubbles.

I needed to see what would happen next. My face pressed on the glass with eagerness.

Danya includes what she was thinking during this scene in a thought bubble and in the text.

Danya includes dialogue in the text.

My eyes were glued to the gorilla. It was the most amazing thing I ever saw. Then the gorilla took its poop and ATE IT!

Danya gives emphasis to words by capitalizing them.

In her illustration, Danya shows us what characters are doing, such as her sister hopping up and down, trying to see.

I hit myself to make sure I wasn't imaging it. Then I screamed loudly, "EEYUW!" I looked at the gorilla again.

EEYEW!

I can't see!

What else do you notice that Danya did as a writer that she learned from mentor texts?

It was as disgusting as a hundred brains in one little case. "Wow, wow, wow!" I shouted. I leaned on the glass harder and harder.

Danya uses a comparison to show the depth of her emotional response.

Zookeeper   My mom
Arden   Me

It started to mind its own business just as I thought it would a while ago. We asked the zookeeper if it was normal. She said it happened every once in a while.

Danya illustrates two scenes on this page: one of her family talking with the zookeeper and one of the gorilla.

 Online Resource 1.1
You can download Danya's book in the online resources.

A Teacher's Guide to Mentor Texts

Excerpts from Alyssa's Feature Article, Grade 4

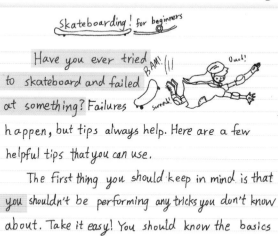

Alyssa writes a *question lead* to draw her readers into the article.

Alyssa uses the pronoun *you* to address her readers directly.

Alyssa includes an illustration that shows what to do and what not to do.

Alyssa defines each stance.

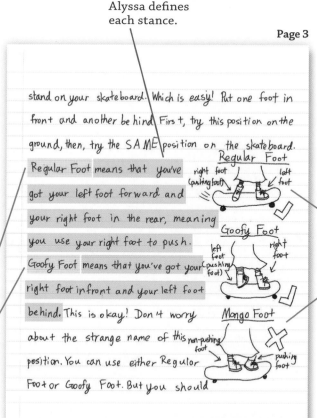

Alyssa uses illustrations to elaborate on her definitions.

Alyssa gives the specific names of skateboarding stances.

What else do you notice that Alyssa did as a writer that she learned from mentor texts?

Page 4

never ever stand in a position that makes your front foot the pushing foot. This position is called the Mongo Foot. Remember to NEVER EVER EVER use the Mongo Foot when you skateboard. It will cause MANY possible dangers. Other than that, be creative, there is no "typical" correct way to stand on a skateboard. Okay, back to the good stuff. To REALLY ride a skateboard, you just get onto it and push. Okay, kidding, nearly that easy, but no. You put your front foot on the skateboard, and push with your back foot. When your skateboard

Get Ready! /// Push... /// Whee!

Alyssa makes humorous asides.

Alyssa capitalizes all the letters in some words to create emphasis.

Alyssa includes a step-by-step illustration.

Page 5

starts moving, quickly put your back foot on your skateboard and let it carry you to paradise. When you slow down, give another quick push with your back foot, get back into position, and let your skateboard help you continue your journey to paradise. Try not to linger with your foot on the ground when the skateboard moves, you'll trip or fall. As a beginner, you will feel scared at some point. If you want to stop, just place your back foot on the ground, and your skateboard will skid to a stop. Do not hesitate while you are stopping, you might

Alyssa elaborates using a series of precise, step-by-step action facts.

Alyssa names her intended audience before giving advice.

Alyssa punctuates dependent clauses with commas.

↓ **Online Resource 1.2**
You can read the rest of Alyssa's feature article in the online resources.

What Will You Learn About How to Use Mentor Texts in This Book?

In the chapters ahead, you'll learn about what it means to read like a writer, and then these five steps for teaching with mentor texts:

STEP 1

Find your own mentor texts.

→

STEP 2

Get to know your mentor texts.

STEP 5

Teach with mentor texts in mini-lessons, small groups, and writing conferences.

STEP 3

Immerse students in mentor texts.

STEP 4

Lead whole-class text study.

Reading Like a Writer

To use mentor texts well in your teaching, it's crucial that you understand the concept of *reading like a writer*.

Reading like a writer is a special kind of close reading that writers do as they read texts. Since being a writer is part of their identity, writers read texts differently than people who don't see themselves in this way. When they read, writers think of themselves as people who are like the authors of the texts they're reading, that is, people who compose texts. Since they see themselves as "insiders" in the process of composing texts, as writers read they notice the things other authors do, such as use interesting craft techniques. Later, they use what they notice in their own writing.

In fact, insiders in any activity experience that activity differently than people who aren't. For example, if you've decided to redesign your kitchen, you notice details about your friends' kitchens you didn't see before. What brand appliances did they install, and how did they arrange them? What kind of tile did they choose for their backsplash? How many cabinets do they have, and how much storage space do they contain? You ask these questions because you're in the process of making your own design decisions for your kitchen-to-be. And many times you'll see a design choice in someone else's kitchen that you'll incorporate in your own.

Understanding what it means to read like a writer will help you be a better writing teacher because:

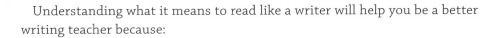

One of your most important goals as a writing teacher is to help students get better at this kind of reading, as experienced writers frequently talk about how reading like a writer is an integral part of their writing lives.

To teach students about crafting techniques in mini-lessons, small-group lessons, and writing conferences, you need to be comfortable with reading like a writer yourself.

Getting better at reading like a writer will also open your eyes when you read to even more of what writers do when they compose texts, and help you develop your repertoire of craft moves you'll draw from when you teach your students.

Q & A

How can you help students develop identities as writers?

> "[T]o read like writers, [children] must perceive themselves as writers."
>
> **Frank Smith (1988)**

Since reading like a writer is something that people who see themselves as writers do, here are some ways you can help your students develop strong writing identities:

* Provide regular time for your students to write across the school year (having a daily writing workshop in your classroom is the best way to do this). Just like children will see themselves as baseball players if they regularly attend baseball practices and play in games, students will come to see themselves as writers if writing is something they do each day and they expect to do in the future.

* Have your students write in real-world genres, ones they're interested in. For example, instead of writing reports, fourth graders can write feature articles like the ones they read in *Highlights* or *Ranger Rick*. Or instead of writing nonfiction pieces, first graders should be writing all-about books like the ones in their classroom libraries. When students are writing in the same genres as other writers, they're more likely to see themselves as writers and try in their own writing what these writers do.

* When you talk about mentor texts, be sure to name the authors of the texts, show a picture of them, and share anything you might know about them. (You can usually find photos and biographical information online.) When students understand texts are written by actual people, they can more easily aspire to be like them.

* Address your students *as writers* when you talk to them as a group. For example, begin mini-lessons by saying, "Writers, today we're going to talk about how to write dialogue in stories." Addressing students like this helps students imagine they really are writers.

* In writing conferences, address students as writers, too. For example, you can begin conferences by asking students, "What are you doing as a writer today?"

* Also in conferences, point out the ways that students already write like the authors of mentor texts, and tell them you're going to teach them to do other things these authors do. Making these direct individualized connections between students and the authors of mentor texts is a powerful way of helping students see themselves as writers!

Quotes from Authors

"Reading is not optional."
—Walter Dean Myers

→ Becoming a writer starts with reading.

"Read like a butterfly, write like a bee."
—Phillip Pullman

→ Like butterflies take nectar from flowers, writers learn about craft from texts. Then, like busy bees, they apply what they learn from their texts to their writing.

"From a really young age, I was reading like a writer. I was reading for the deep understanding of the literature; not simply to hear the story but to understand how the author got the story on the page."
—Jacqueline Woodson

→ Jacqueline Woodson developed the habit of reading like a writer as a child and studied texts to see how authors composed them.

"The best teachers of writing are the great writers themselves. If we read enough, certain truths become self-evident. There are certain things great writers always do, and certain things they never do, and a proper study of their works will show us what these are."
—Madeleine L'Engle

→ We need "great writers" in our lives if we're going to be writers, too. They are important writing teachers for us.

"If you don't have time to read, you don't have the time (or the tools) to write. Simple as that."
—Stephen King

→ Reading gives writers the "tools" they need to write. You can't be a writer without being a reader.

"I really do one thing. I read books . . . I write books. I think about books. It's one job."
—Toni Morrison

→ For most people, their job is a central part of their identity. For Toni Morrison, the job of being a writer involves reading as much as writing. To her, reading and writing are inseparable activities.

Three Ways to Read Like a Writer

1. Writers read like a writer as part of their reading lives.

The first way that writers read like writers happens naturally whenever they read texts. As they read, writers notice all sorts of things about what other writers do—sometimes without even being conscious they're doing so—and later draw upon this bank of knowledge when they write.

For example, I've picked up many craft techniques while reading without even realizing it and now I use them when I write. You may have noticed I directly address you, the reader, in many sections of this book. I choose to write in second person because it creates a friendly, personal tone in my writing. How did I learn this technique? I must have picked it up from the authors of professional books I've read who often use this technique, as well as authors of many other kinds of texts I've read.

• **WORDS FROM A TEACHING MENTOR** •

> *"Students need to read as a writer—slowly, carefully, sometimes enviously, always asking, 'How did they do that?' The best 'rules' we can learn are those we derive from reading authors we admire."*

Tom Newkirk (2021)

Reflect on Your Writing Life

Read through a piece of your writing and look for craft moves you used. Which ones do you have no memory of learning from a teacher, which you probably learned about as you've read? Take a moment to marvel at how your experiences as a reader have helped you be a better writer!

2. Writers read like a writer to build a craft repertoire.

This way of reading like writers is more intentional and involves studying one or several texts to build a repertoire of crafting techniques. Usually, writers do this because there's an aspect of craft they want to get better at in their writing. For example, a writer who wants to write successfully in a new genre will read several examples of the genre and notice the typical craft techniques writers use in this kind of writing, such as setting in historical fiction or counterargument in argument writing, so they can do the same. Or a writer who wants to create more voice in their writing might study a stack of texts to see what kinds of craft moves the authors used to give their writing *voice*, such as capitalizing all the letters of a word or phrase to signal the reader to give it emphasis, or writing short sentences to let readers know to give them a beat when they read them.

Although I have been a writer of professional books about the teaching of writing for twenty years, when I wrote my first Classroom Essentials book, *A Teacher's Guide to Writing Conferences*, I knew right away I would need to build a new repertoire of craft techniques. One of the distinguishing features of the books in this series is the way information is conveyed in striking ways in a wide variety of text features. Since I had not written a book like this before, I studied numerous books that contained interesting text features. Some of these features included:

Cartoons that bring conversations to life.	"Q & A" boxes to answer frequently asked questions about the topic of the book.	"Words from a Teaching Mentor" boxes to highlight what literacy leaders say about the topic.	"Tips" boxes to give advice on how to do something.	"Teaching Point Library" boxes that list resources for further study.

As I wrote *A Teacher's Guide to Writing Conferences*, I used all these text features and more. And in the process of writing the book you're now reading, I studied more books—including all the books in the Classroom Essentials series that came out after my first one—to build my repertoire even further.

Let's step back and name some important features of the experience I had as I read like a writer to build my craft repertoire:

I have an identity as writer of professional books. This identity is the foundation of why I read like a writer.

I gathered a stack of texts to intentionally study an aspect of craft—text features.

When I noticed a text feature, I named what the writer did.

I thought about why the author chose to use these features.

Finally, I used the crafting techniques that I noticed in my own writing.

Reflect on Your Writing Life

Think about times in your writing life when you read like a writer to build up your own repertoire of craft moves, and think about what you did as part of these experiences. For example, perhaps you were asked to give a toast at a wedding, so in the weddings you attended beforehand, or the movies or TV shows you watched that featured weddings, you listened especially carefully to the toasts to get a sense of the things you could do in your own.

3. Writers read like a writer to study a specific craft technique.

This way of reading like a writer is also intentional. While writing a draft, writers use many craft techniques. However, they may not know how to use a technique, such as flashback. Or they might be having trouble with a technique—such a writing a particular kind of lead to a piece. To help them use a technique well, writers study a text in which the author uses it effectively.

For example, when I wrote my first book, *How's It Going? A Practical Guide to Conferring with Student Writers* (2000), I wanted to include transcripts of conferences I had with students in the text (this was before it was possible to include links to online video of conferences!). However, I didn't know how to introduce a transcript. For help with this, I went to Georgia Heard's classic book on teaching poetry, *For the Good of the Earth and Sun* (1989), because I remembered she included transcripts of conferences. Here's how she introduced one of her conferences:

> It is afternoon in a classroom in Queens. Most students are hunched over papers, writing; some are looking at the wall or out the window . . . As I look around the room I spot Jason. He has written three lines, and pencil is down. We walk up and crouch next to him.

As I read Georgia's beautiful introduction to her conference with Jason, I noticed several things she did as a writer:

1	2
Georgia establishes the setting of the conference.	She introduces us to the student she's going to confer with.

3	4
She tells us something about what Jason is doing.	She describes what she and the teacher she was with did before the conference started.

With these craft moves in mind, I could now envision how to write introductions to the conferences in my book. Here's one of them:

> Let's take a look at a conference in which a student set the conference agenda. It was an early October morning in Jennifer Geller's second-grade classroom at P.S. 6 in Manhattan. We knelt down to confer with Becky, who was working on revising her story about her sleepover party.

Reflect on Your Writing Life

When have you wanted to use a craft technique in a piece of writing, but you weren't sure of how to do it well? Did you find a text and study it to see how the author did what you wanted to do? What did you learn?

Q & A

Why isn't this copying?

You might be wondering if I "copied" Georgia Heard's way of introducing a conference transcript. The answer is no.

If I had copied Georgia's introduction word for word to introduce my conference, then I rightly could have been accused of copying her work.

Instead, I noticed the craft moves that Georgia used to write her introduction, and then used them myself. These craft moves are not owned by Georgia—she probably saw another writer use them before she wrote her book and decided to use them herself. In turn, I used these same craft moves—and someone who reads my introduction might do the same. In this way, craft moves are passed from one writer to another to another, because they are all in the habit of reading like a writer when they read texts.

No one has a unique writing style. Just like people talk in similar ways to the people who they interact with regularly, writers write like the people they read. A writer's style is an amalgam of the crafting techniques they encounter in the texts they read and study in their life.

Let's name some important features of the experience I had as I read like a writer to study a specific craft technique:

1

I had a new identity as writer of professional books and was highly motivated to learn how to write my first book well.

2

I was in the midst of writing a draft, dealing with all the usual challenges that writers face.

3

I was having a problem with a specific crafting technique— how to introduce a section.

4

I found a text in which the author used this crafting technique.

5

I studied how the author used the technique and named what she did.

6

Finally, I used what I learned in my own writing.

Teaching Implications

Now that you have a clearer understanding of what it means to read like a writer, you're ready to consider its implications for the teaching you'll be doing with mentor texts, implications you'll learn about in the remainder of the book:

1

Students will read like writers when they see themselves as writers, and when they regularly write.

2

To support the kind of reading like a writer students will do as a natural part of their writing lives, make sure they're reading well-written texts that are like the kinds of writing they do in writing workshop, both during the workshop and across the school day.

3

To help your students learn to read like a writer to build their craft repertoires, you'll need to give them some support. You'll do this in whole-class studies of mentor texts in your craft units of study.

4

Just like adult writers, students sometimes struggle with various aspects of writing (e.g., leads, transitions, writing with detail, conventions). Sometimes you'll address these directly in your craft and convention mini-lessons, small-group lessons, and writing conferences. You'll also do this by helping students study mentor texts themselves.

Reading Like a Writer

Try Reading Like a Writer Yourself

If you are new to the concept of reading like a writer, there are some exercises you can do to try it out. Even if you already have some experience, trying these exercises can help you get better at reading like a writer:

Practice reading like a writer to build a repertoire of craft techniques by reading a text of your choice—preferably a genre you enjoy writing in yourself or hope to write in—and as you read, notice some of the craft moves the author makes. Once you've found several interesting moves, name what you think the writer is doing in each of them and why.

Try the same, but this time with a group of colleagues, as you'll collectively notice more crafting techniques and have more insights into them than you would by yourself! Read the text and share out the interesting craft moves you noticed. Together, discuss what the author did as a writer in each of these parts.

Pick one of the craft techniques that you (or your colleagues) have noticed, and try it out in your own writing.

Practice reading like a writer to study a specific craft technique by looking at how a writer uses one technique in a text. Choose one you would like to try yourself or one that you've noticed your students are drawn to, such as writing a good lead or ending, or writing a description of a character, place, or object, and so on.

Try the same, but with a group of colleagues.

Take what you've learned from studying a specific craft technique, and try it out in your own writing.

Reading Like a Writer

STEP 1

Find Your Own Mentor Texts

The first step you'll take to teach with mentor texts is to find good ones. There are several things to consider as you select texts that will be just right for teaching your students how to craft their writing.

What Texts Will You Need?

You'll need mentor texts you can use in each unit of study that's part of your year-long writing curriculum:

For *genre study*, you'll need a stack (several texts) of each genre to share with your students—you'll need how-to books for your how-to book study, feature articles for your feature article study, and so on.

For *craft study* in which students get to choose their own genre (Glover 2019), you'll need texts that contain the kinds of craft techniques that are the focus of the study. For example, in an illustration study, you'll need texts with different kinds of interesting illustrations. Or in a voice study, you'll need texts in which the authors use a variety of voice techniques. Although you might include texts that you've already used (or will use) in your genre studies, you do not need examples of every genre your students choose to write. That's because craft techniques are not genre specific. For example, in a voice study, you can teach a student how to capitalize all the letters in a word to signal to the reader to give that word emphasis by showing them a nonfiction book, even though they're writing short fiction.

• WORDS FROM A TEACHING MENTOR •

"Collecting a handful of mentor texts, and keeping them as resources for students, is like gathering a multitude of teachers into your classroom."

Georgia Heard (2013)

How Many Texts Will You Need?

You'll need a stack of several (at least three or four) texts for each unit you teach. Students will learn more about craft when they have several texts to study, especially when the texts are written by different authors who have different repertoires of crafting techniques. Sometimes you'll use a text in several units (for example, you might use Ibtihaj Muhammad's *The Proudest Blue: A Story of Hijab and Family* in a genre study of short fiction, as well as in a voice study), so that will cut down the total number of texts you'll need for the school year. Over time, you'll continue to gather texts, as finding good mentor texts is part of the lifework of being a writing teacher!

> **Tip**
>
> → When you have a *process* study in your curriculum—a unit of study in which you teach students how to navigate a stage of the writing process (Glover 2019)—you'll use *process* mentor texts. For example, in a unit of study on launching writers' notebooks, a tool writers use during the rehearsal stage of the writing process, you'll have some sample writers' notebooks to show students, most likely your own and perhaps those of students you taught in previous years. Or in a *revision* study, you'll teach students what revision looks like by showing them drafts with revisions visible on them, again probably your own and those of students.

It's a good idea to take stock of your collection of mentor texts at the beginning of the school year to see if there are any gaps. If there are, then you can keep an eye out for texts that can fill them. Otherwise, you risk starting a unit of study by scrambling to find mentor texts for it at the last moment.

To take stock of your collection, use this Mentor Text Planning Form (you can download the form from the Online Teaching Resources):

 **Online Resource 3.1**
Mentor Text Planning Form

Mentor Text Planning Form

Unit of Study	Mentor Texts I Plan to Use
	1.
	2.
	3.
	4.
	1.
	2.
	3.
	4.
	1.
	2.
	3.
	4.
	1.
	2.
	3.
	4.

May be photocopied for classroom use. ©2022 by Carl Anderson from
A Teacher's Guide to Mentor Texts, Grades K–5. Portsmouth, NH: Heinemann.

Choosing Mentor Texts

There are several questions to consider as you choose texts for your collection:

 Can students see their lives reflected in the texts?

↓

Rudine Sims Bishop (1990) writes about the importance of texts being "mirrors" that reflect students' life experiences and interests. This cannot be overstated. With mentor texts that are mirrors, students are more inspired to write and more motivated to study how authors craft their work.

It is essential that your narrative mentor texts feature characters that look like the children in your classroom and community. When students read about characters from diverse backgrounds—different races, ethnicities, classes, cultures, religions, languages, genders, sexual orientations, abilities, and family histories—they feel seen. If children meet characters who look, speak, eat, dress, dance, sing, pray, study and play like they do, they learn that they—and their stories—matter. Diverse mentor texts not only make all students visible; they also teach children to empathize, a key tool in a writers' quiver.

Likewise, your informational nonfiction and opinion texts should focus on topics that reflect your students' interests and concerns—from Minecraft to bullying—validating that these interests and concerns are worthwhile topics to write about.

• WORDS FROM A TEACHING MENTOR •

"Literature transforms human experience and reflects it back to us, and in that reflection we can see our lives and experiences as part of the larger human experience. Reading then becomes a means of self-affirmation, and readers often seek their mirrors in books."

Rudine Sims Bishop (1990)

• WORDS FROM A WRITER •

"It wasn't that [my] teachers were bad. From what I can remember, they were pretty good. It was about the selection of books. It was about not seeing my young life reflected back to me: my family dynamics, the noise and complexities of my neighborhood, the things I loved, like ice cream trucks and Kool-Aid."

Jason Reynolds (2019)

(2)

Can students see new possibilities for their lives and the world in the texts? →

Rudine Sims Bishop (1990) also writes that texts can be "windows" and "sliding glass doors" for children. Peering through windows allows them to envision new paths ahead. Walking through open doors, they can venture onto those paths. These mentor texts give students reasons to write, propel them to investigate the craft moves that drew them in, and drive them to try those techniques in their own writing.

For example, stories that feature characters confronting family, friendship, school, community, or global problems help students imagine that they, too, can write stories in which characters try to change the world. Informational nonfiction and opinion texts that wrestle with difficult issues inspire students to do the same in their pieces.

• **WORDS FROM A WRITER** •

"I'm talking with a girl. She's at that age where the edges of the woman she will become are just starting to press against her baby-round face, and I will make a fantastic world, a cartography of all the places a girl like her can go, and put it in a book. The rest of the work lies in the imagination of everyone else along the way, the publishers, librarians, teachers, parents, and all of us, to put that book in her hands."

Christopher Meyers (2014)

(3) **Is there diverse representation among the authors of the texts?** →

It is also important that your mentor texts are written by authors with different backgrounds, perspectives, and experiences. Texts written by a diverse group of authors make it possible for all students to imagine themselves as writers.

• **WORDS FROM A TEACHING MENTOR** •

"Books are sometimes windows, offering views of worlds that may be real or imagined, familiar or strange. These windows are also sliding glass doors, and readers only have to walk through in imagination to become part of whatever world has been created and recreated by the author."

Rudine Sims Bishop (1990)

• **WORDS FROM A TEACHING MENTOR** •

"What writing—and whose voices—do you hold up as mentors of excellent writing?"

Tricia Ebarvia (2017)

Will your students enjoy reading the texts?

Students will be more interested in studying a text when it's one that in some way moved them as they read it—an all-about nonfiction book that wows them with its interesting facts, a memoir that makes them laugh or feel sad, an argument that gets them thinking about an issue.

Do you see lots of potential teaching points in the texts?

Your mentor texts should contain the kinds of crafting techniques you want to teach in your units of study. You can learn what these techniques are by becoming familiar with the writing standards for your grade level, and by reading through your units of study guides. If you're projecting—or designing—your own units of study (Glover and Berry 2012), your mentor texts will be your most important source of craft teaching points. It's important to understand that you *don't* need a different mentor text for each crafting technique you want to teach, as each mentor text contains numerous techniques.

Can students comprehend the texts or understand the texts when read to them?

If texts are too difficult for students to read, it will be hard for students to notice the craft techniques the authors of the texts used and to understand why they used the techniques.

Do the texts have a grade-appropriate amount of text in each section?

The amount of text should feel attainable to your students as writers.

Do the texts represent different levels of challenges for students with varying skill as writers?

When you're teaching less experienced writers, you'll need texts that contain simpler craft moves, and with more experienced writers, ones that are more sophisticated.

Do you love the texts?

When you love a text, you'll read and talk about it with excitement and passion. Your enthusiasm for a text will be contagious with your students.

Finding Good Mentor Texts

There are many sources of mentor texts. You'll be able to find many of them in your classroom or school:

Your classroom library has many potential mentor texts.

For example, classroom libraries in primary grades contain narrative and informational nonfiction picture books that can be used as mentor texts, and the magazines like *Time for Kids* that upper-grade teachers subscribe to for their classes contain potential mentor texts in many genres.

Ask your colleagues to share the ones they use.

For teachers who are new to a grade, this can be an excellent way to get a starter set of mentor texts.

Your school library contains many potential mentor texts.

Ask your school librarian to help you with your search—they love to be a useful resource for classroom teachers.

Children's magazines contain a wide variety of genres that can be excellent mentor texts.

For example, *Highlights* and the Cricket Media family of magazines (*Click, Ask, Spider, Cricket*, etc.) contain well-written short fiction and informational nonfiction texts for children in elementary school grades.

Do an internet search.

For example, Googling "sources of writing mentor texts" will turn up numerous links to websites where educators suggest favorite mentor texts.

Visit websites dedicated to sharing lists of great texts.

For example, movingwriters.org and diversebooks.org.

Some published writing curriculums come with mentor texts.

For example, mentor texts are bundled with Lucy Calkins' Units of Study series and some can be downloaded as PDFs from the online resources for the series.

Read professional books.

Many professional books on the teaching of craft, such as Ralph Fletcher's *What a Writer Needs* (2013), Stacey Shubitz's *Craft Moves* (2016), and Melissa Stewart and Marlene Correia's *5 Kinds of Nonfiction* (2021) either discuss great mentor texts or contain a list of suggested mentor texts, or both.

Look for collections of particular genres written for children:

There are numerous collections of poetry written for children.

Garth Sundem's *Real Kids, Real Stories, Real Change* (2010) is a collection of profiles of activist kids from around the world. (He has several other collections of profiles, with different themes.)

The Chicken Soup series also contains many wonderfully written narratives (e.g., *Chicken Soup for the Preteen Soul* [Canfield, Hanson, and Hanson 2021]).

Many children's authors have written memoir, including Jacqueline Woodson (*Brown Girl Dreaming* [2016]) and Ralph Fletcher (*Marshfield Dreams* [2012]) and short fiction, such as Jason Reynold's *Look Both Ways* (2019).

Q & A

Can I use my own writing as a mentor text?

Yes! Using your own writing has many benefits. When you share your own writing with your students, you'll find students will love what you write and will see you as a "real" writer, which will give you more credibility as a writing teacher. Also, when you write a mentor text, you can embed some of the craft techniques you want to teach students into your text, and you'll be able to explain to students why and how you decided to use them. As you try these craft moves in your writing, you'll be reminded of how challenging these moves can be, which will help you teach with more empathy and understanding. Finally, some kinds of writing are hard to find for kids, such as literary essay, so writing your own is one of the best ways to get some for your collection. In fact, if your grade-level colleagues each write one of these hard-to-find genres—and you share them—you'll quickly have more than enough for your collection.

Q & A

Can I use student writing as mentor texts?

Of course! Students enjoy seeing other students' writing. And since student writing is closer to their level than the writing done by adults, they will feel more confident they can try out the craft techniques they see fellow students use.

As you read published student work at the end of a unit, be on the lookout for student writing you can copy and save to use as mentor texts in the future. Most students will be honored to give permission for you to save their work and use it in this way!

As you gather student writing, look for a range of samples, not just the strongest examples. By having a range, you'll be able to match students up to student-written mentor texts that will be a reasonable next step for them, wherever they currently are as writers.

Organizing Your Collection of Mentor Texts

It's important to have a special place for your mentor texts in your class-room. This will help you find the texts that you need for mini-lessons, small-group lessons, or writing conferences when you need them. And students will be able to find a mentor text when they need one, too.

Here are two ways teachers have organized their mentor texts:

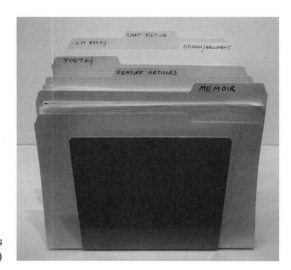

**Folders of Texts
(upper-grade classroom)**

Bins of texts (primary classroom)

Take It to Your Classroom

Here are tips to help you get started gathering your collection of mentor texts or to help you assess the collection of texts you already have. You can do this work individually or together with your colleagues on your grade level.

If You're Starting a Collection of Mentor Texts:

1

List the units of study in your writing curriculum on the Mentor Text Planning Form.

2

Use the list of sources of mentor texts described in this chapter to help you identify where to go to find possible mentor texts.

3

As you find texts, use the criteria for choosing texts described in this chapter to help you decide which ones to make part of your collection.

4

Add texts you think meet the criteria to the Mentor Text Planning Form.

Tip

→ If you're teaching online, some picture books are available as e-books that you can download using the Kindle or iBooks app. You can also download articles from the websites of children's magazines and put them in folders on your desktop for each unit of study. Or you could take pictures of a text with your smartphone, email them to yourself, and then drag them to the appropriate folder.

If You're Assessing an Already Existing Collection of Mentor Texts:

1

List the units of study in your writing curriculum and the mentor texts you already have for each unit on the Mentor Text Planning Form.

2

Use the criteria for choosing texts described in this chapter to think about your mentor texts. Which criteria have you satisfied, and which ones have you not? Which sources of mentor texts described in this chapter can you go to find texts to fill in these gaps?

3

Are there any units of study for which you don't have enough mentor texts, or don't have any at all? If so, which sources of mentor texts can you go to find texts for these units?

Step 1: Find Your Own Mentor Texts

STEP 2

Get to Know Your Mentor Texts

You want your mentor texts to be *versatile*, that is, texts that enable you to teach students about many craft techniques and conventions. For example, in her book *What You Know by Heart* (2002), Katie Wood Ray lists 100 teaching points she found in Cynthia Rylant's *The Whales* (1996)!

Getting to know your mentor texts well is important. Once you've done this work, you can use a text to teach in a wide variety of mini-lessons, small groups, and writing conferences.

Analyze a Text for Multiple Teaching Points

There are two steps to finding multiple teaching points in a mentor text:

1 Read the text, and as you read, be on the lookout for craft techniques that stand out to you. For example, you might notice an interesting lead, a gorgeous simile, or an interesting text feature. By the time you finish reading through the text, you'll probably find several crafting techniques you could use in your teaching.

2 Read through the texts several more times, each time using one of the qualities, or traits, of writing as a lens to help you identify additional craft moves you can add to your teaching repertoire. These include:

Focus, or developing a single topic or idea throughout a piece.

Structure, the parts or sections of a text, and how they're organized.

Detail, the particulars or specifics of a piece of writing.

Voice, the sound or cadence of a piece of writing.

Conventions, which include punctuation, capitalization, and grammar.

Q & A

What if I use different terms to describe the qualities of writing?

There are several versions of the qualities of writing in the professional literature that use other words to describe them. The good news is the words on one list are sometimes synonyms of those on others and can be used interchangeably. And sometimes a word on one list is inclusive of several words on another.

Here is a chart that you can use as a translation guide:

Qualities of Writing Translation Guide

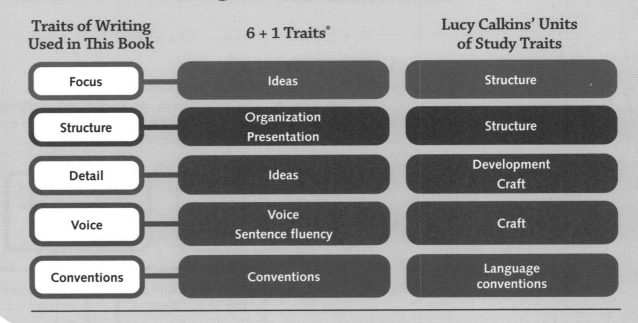

Traits of Writing Used in This Book	6 + 1 Traits®	Lucy Calkins' Units of Study Traits
Focus	Ideas	Structure
Structure	Organization Presentation	Structure
Detail	Ideas	Development Craft
Voice	Voice Sentence fluency	Craft
Conventions	Conventions	Language conventions

Analyzing a Text for Focus

One of the challenges student writers face is learning how to focus their writing:

> **Primary writers sometimes write about a different topic on each page of their books and need to learn to develop one topic across a book.**

> **Student writers of all ages sometimes write bed-to-bed pieces and need to learn to focus by writing about part of a topic.**

> **Students also need to learn they can focus a piece on an idea about their topic.**

With these needs in mind, when you analyze a text for focus, ask yourself, "In which way did the author focus this text? Does the author write about the same topic on each page? About part of the topic? About an idea about the topic?" For some texts, it's possible you could say the author focused the text in two or even all three ways, which will allow you to use the same text to teach students who have different focus needs.

You can also use the lens of focus to analyze the illustrations in a picture book or an illustrated text like a feature article, which will equip you to show students different ways to focus their own illustrations:

> **Illustrators sometimes zoom in on their subject, filling the page with it so its details are visible.**

> **Conversely, illustrators sometimes zoom out in an illustration, showing their subject in its larger context.**

Analyzing a Text for Structure

Students need to learn how to structure their writing. Structure refers to the parts of the piece and how they go together to develop a topic. When you analyze a text for structure, these are some of the aspects of structure to pay attention to:

Genres have parts that are their basic building blocks—for example, narratives are made up of scenes, informational pieces have sections and text features, and opinion pieces have reasons. Genres also have parts writers may or may not choose to include—for example, flashback in narrative genres or a how-to section in nonfiction genres.

These parts are ordered in genre-specific ways—narrative scenes are ordered in time, informational nonfiction and opinion, logically.

Genres also have parts that perform special roles, such as leads and endings.

Writers have ways to signal that some parts are especially important in developing the focus of a piece, such as developing them ("stretching them out") more fully than others.

Writers use transitions to signal readers where parts begin and end.

You can also use the lens of structure to help you think about the illustrations in a text. Some genres, such as those in the category of informational nonfiction, have numerous kinds of text features such as labeled diagrams, fun facts, and so on.

54

Analyzing a Text for Detail

You have probably urged your students to add detail to their writing many times in your teaching! Detail refers to the particulars, or specifics, of a piece of writing.

For students to learn to write with detail well, they need to understand several dimensions of this quality of writing, dimensions you should be on the lookout for when you analyze a text:

Detail is genre specific. That is, writers use certain kinds of details depending upon the genres they're writing. For example, in narrative genres, writers include character actions, thoughts and feelings, dialogue, and character and setting description. In informational nonfiction, writers include different kinds of facts, such as action facts, descriptive facts, and number facts, and so on. And in persuasive genres, writers include examples, anecdotes, text citations, and others.

Writers weave the various kinds of details together in the sections of their pieces.

In picture books and in illustrated texts, illustrators include many of these kinds of details in the pictures.

Writers use specific nouns, verbs, adjectives, and adverbs in their details.

Writers sometimes use transitions to connect details to each other in a section.

Analyzing a Text for Voice

Students have a lot to learn about giving their writing voice. Voice is a quality of writing that refers to the sound of human speech coming through the text, or the personality of the writer or narrator. Writers use voice techniques to help them get across what they're trying to say, just as there are many ways we use our voice when we speak to communicate.

Writers embed various signals in texts to cue readers about how to read them. These signals include punctuation (exclamation points, ellipses, dashes), as well as how words are formatted (boldface type, all caps, italics).

Another way that writers signal how to read a part of a text is by using certain sentence structures readers know should be read in a certain way (for example, intentional repetition of a word or phrase signals that the repeated word or phrase should be emphasized).

Writers also give their writing voice by how they address readers with the pronoun *you*, which creates a conversational tone. Similarly, using the first person creates a sense of intimacy. On the other hand, using the third person creates a more formal tone in a text.

A Teacher's Guide to Mentor Texts

Analyzing a Text for Conventions

For those of you who learned about conventions from grammar textbooks when you were children, the idea of using mentor texts to teach them may be surprising. But what better way to teach conventions than to look at the ways an author of a favorite text does so? When conventions are presented in this way, the subject becomes much more appealing to young writers.

As you read a mentor text, pay attention to the many punctuation, capitalization, grammar, and paragraphing conventions the author uses so you'll be able to show these conventions when you teach.

→ **For more information about the qualities of writing, read my book *Assessing Writers* (Anderson 2005).**

Analyzing *Jabari Jumps* for Multiple Teaching Points

Gaia Cornwall's *Jabari Jumps* (2017), a story about a boy who overcomes his nervousness about jumping off a high diving board, is beloved by teachers and students alike. By using the qualities of writing to analyze just a few of the pages in this picture book, you'll see the book contains a wide variety of craft techniques.

Focus → The author focuses this story on a small part of Jabari's day (we commonly refer to this kind of focus in narrative as a "small moment" story).

Structure → The author writes a dialogue lead, the content of which puts the story in motion.

"I'm jumping off the diving board today," Jabari told his dad. "Really?" said his dad.

Focus ↓

In this illustration, the author zooms in onto Jabari, his dad, and little sister. We don't even see Jabari and his dad's entire bodies!

Detail ↓

In the illustrations, we see many character details: the characters' faces, clothing, sunglasses, and swim goggles. We also see background setting.

Conventions → The author punctuates the dialogue with quotation marks and puts the comma and question marks that end the lines of dialogue before the second quotation mark.

Structure

↓

Readers transition from one part of the story to the next by turning the pages of the book.

Detail

↓

The author uses the transition *then* and the coordinating conjunction *and* to link character actions together.

Focus

↓

The author zooms out in this illustration so we can see the swimming pool that is at the center of this story, as well as Jabari, his dad, and sister viewing it.

Detail

↓

The author writes a series of character actions, one made by the main character and then several by the secondary characters.

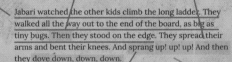

Jabari watched the other kids climb the long ladder. They walked all the way out to the end of the board, as big as tiny bugs. Then they stood on the edge. They spread their arms and bent their knees. And sprang up! up! up! And then they dove down, down, down.

Splash!

"Looks easy," Jabari said.

But when his dad squeezed his hand, Jabari squeezed back.

Voice

↓

The author gives emphasis to the word *splash* in several ways: she puts the word by itself on the line, italicizes it, and uses an exclamation mark.

Detail

↓

The author uses precise verbs.

Voice

↓

The author repeats the words *up* and *down* three times each in immediate succession so readers will give them emphasis when they read them (epizeuxis).

Detail

Facial expressions give information about characters' feelings.

Detail

The author writes a series of two main character actions.

Jabari stood at the bottom of the ladder. He looked up.

"You can go before me if you want," he told the kid behind him.

"I need to think about what kind of special jump I'm going to do."

Jabari thought and thought.

Structure

The author does a moment-by-moment series of three illustrations to illustrate a sequence of events.

Conventions

The author begins sentences with capital letters and ends them with punctuation marks (periods).

Voice

↓

The author italicizes this thought to give it emphasis.

Voice

↓

The author repeats the word *up* separated by the word *and* to emphasize the motion (diacope).

Reread these pages from *Jabari Jumps*—or if you have a copy of the book, reread the whole book. Where else do you see the author use these crafting techniques? What other ones can you find?

Detail

↓

The author includes two of Jabari's thoughts.

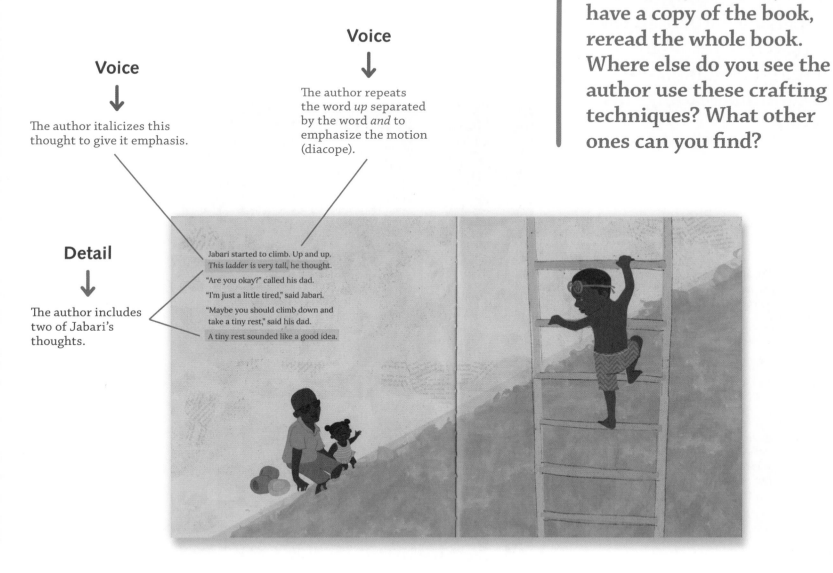

Jabari started to climb. Up and up. *This ladder is very tall,* he thought.

"Are you okay?" called his dad.

"I'm just a little tired," said Jabari.

"Maybe you should climb down and take a tiny rest," said his dad.

A tiny rest sounded like a good idea.

You can find a copy of "Surprising Saturn" in the online resources. Print it out and read it before you continue reading this section.

Analyzing "Surprising Saturn" for Multiple Teaching Points

In this feature article from *Ask* magazine, the author, Liz Huyck, uses numerous craft techniques:

Focus

The article focuses on part of the larger topic of the solar system.

Structure

The lead is a narrative scene, and takes the reader (addressed as "you") on a journey to the topic.

Focus

The illustration of Saturn is a close-up view of the planet.

The author includes several cartoons as text features that parallel the content of the lead.

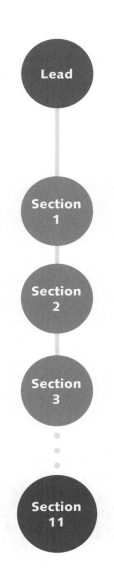

Lead

Section 1

Section 2

Section 3

Section 11

The article begins with a lead, followed by a series of sections.

Structure
↓
The first section gives a general overview of the topic.

Focus
↓
This text feature zooms out so readers can see the entire solar system and Saturn's place within it.

Detail
↓
The author includes many number facts in the text to describe size, time, as well as distance and temperature.

Detail
↓
The author includes a definition of a term.

Detail
↓
The author enhances a descriptive fact with comparisons.

Structure
↓
This text feature is a cutaway drawing that allows us to see the interior of Saturn.

ROCKY PLANETS   GAS PLANETS

Mercury Venus Earth Mars Jupiter Saturn Uranus Neptune

This shows how the planets compare in size (but distances are squashed).

Nine Earths could fit across Saturn.

Welcome to Saturn

Saturn is the sixth planet from the sun, and the second largest planet in our solar system. It's 95 times more massive than Earth, and 9 times as wide.

A year on Saturn (the time it takes to go around the sun once) is 29.5 Earth years long. But the days are short. Saturn is spinning very quickly, so it has a new day every 10.5 hours.

Saturn is very far away. It orbits about 870 million miles (1,400 million km) from the sun. Even a very fast spaceship would take 7 or 8 years to get there. Cell phone signals, traveling at the speed of light, take over an hour to make the trip. So phone calls to Saturn would have long pauses.

The planet gets its name from Saturn, the Roman god of agriculture and father of Jupiter. Saturday is also named for him, so Saturday is a great day to look at Saturn.

Wash behind your rings!

It Has No Surface

Like Jupiter, Neptune, and Uranus, Saturn is a gas planet. That means it has no solid surface—it's a big ball of cloud. So after you've come all this way, you won't be able to land on it!

You also probably shouldn't try to fly through it. Even though it's made of gas, Saturn is huge and has strong gravity. If a spaceship tried to fly through, gas molecules would rub against the ship and heat it up—a lot. Then the force of all the gas pressing in would crush it like a tin can.

What kind of gas is it? Saturn is mostly hydrogen, helium, and water vapor, with clouds of ammonia and other chemicals. Near Saturn's center, the pressure is so intense that hydrogen is squashed into a metallic liquid. At the very center, it may have a small core of rock, like the pit in a cherry. But we don't know for sure.

It Would Float in a Bathtub

Saturn is enormous, but it's not very dense. It's kind of like a foamy marshmallow, or a big cloud of haze. So if you could find a bathtub big enough, Saturn would float!

Hydrogen, helium, and other gases

Possibly a small solid core?

Metallic hydrogen

Layers of Cloud

Saturn has layers of gas, swirling around like a big gassy onion. There may be a small solid core in the middle, under a blanket of metallic hydrogen.

Um...Maybe there's a store on Jupiter?

Asteroids Ahead

ask 7

Reread "Surprising Saturn." Where else do you see the author use these crafting techniques? What other ones can you find?

Detail →

Detail ↓

The author uses the transition *and* to start the third sentence in a list of three related sentences.

The author uses the coordinating conjuction *but* to link this sentence to the previous one.

Structure ↓

The author uses subheadings to help readers transition from part to part and to preview the content of each section.

Voice ↓

By asking the reader a question and then answering it, the author creates a friendly, intimate tone.

Conventions →

The author uses commas to set off an introductory word, and to punctuate the compound sentence.

Conventions

The author uses dashes and commas before descriptive clauses in sentences.

Structure → The author writes a chronology of events in this section.

Detail

The author includes action facts to describe what Saturn's moons do.

Structure

The author uses the trading cards text feature to elaborate on this section.

Many Moons

Saturn is rich in rings, and also in moons—it has at least 62. There are eight big ones and dozens of smaller ones. Some orbit close to the planet. Some are millions of miles away. And some tumble around in the rings.

Saturn's moons are mostly ice and rock dust. Most are quite small, less than 100 miles (160 km) across. The small moons inside Saturn's rings are called shepherd moons. They make gaps in the rings by sweeping up ice. They also make waves. The rings are also full of tiny "moonlets," the beginnings of new moons.

A few groups of small moons orbit quite far from Saturn. These distant moons are probably pieces of captured asteroids—giant balls of ice and rock that wandered too close to the planet.

Two moons, Titan and Enceladus, have underground oceans beneath icy outer shells. Titan has methane lakes and even an atmosphere. Scientists think these moons might be a good place to look for life. They're working on probes to explore them close up.

62 moons! That's a lot of cheese!

Saturn's second-largest moon, Rhea, in front of its largest, Titan.

Or ice!

World's largest snowball!

Moon fight!

TETHYS
MOON OF SATURN
Named for: Goddess of fresh water
Miles across: 662 (1,065 km)
Voted: Shiniest
Saturn's fifth-largest moon has a bright, icy surface marked by many craters from space rocks, including a large one on one side.

HYPERION
MOON OF SATURN
Named for: God of watchfulness
Miles across: 168 (270 km)
Voted: Most spongy
This small, lumpy moon is mostly ice. It may be the remnant of a larger moon that broke up. It is full of holes, like a huge icy sponge.

ARE WE THERE YET?

You asked that last year.

10

Exploring Saturn

People have been looking at Saturn since ancient times. To the naked eye, Saturn is just a bright dot in the night sky. The first person to spot Saturn's rings was the astronomer Galileo, looking through one of the first telescopes. Galileo wasn't quite sure what the bulges were.

In 1656, an astronomer named Christiaan Huygens figured out that the bulges were rings.

A few years later, Giovanni Cassini saw that Saturn has many rings, not just one.

In 1980, the Voyager 1 spacecraft snapped pictures of Saturn and some of its moons as it zipped by on its way to the outer planets. In 2004, Saturn got its very own visitor, the Cassini spacecraft, named after the astronomer). After a 7 year journey, it spent 13 years orbiting Saturn and taking pictures. It also took measurements that told scientists what Saturn and the rings were made of and how they moved. In 2017, Cassini ended its mission by falling into Saturn. The next mission to Saturn will be a robotic drone called Dragonfly. It will explore the moon Titan and look for signs of life. It is scheduled to launch sometime in the 2030s.

Saturn and its largest moon, Titan.

I'm going to find moon #63!

Early astronomers used long telescopes to get a better look at Saturn.

The Cassini space probe flew around Saturn and its moons for many years, snapping pictures and sampling the rings.

A Saturn moon! At last!

Wait, we have to go back! I forgot the camera.

11

Structure

↓

The author transitions into events by telling the years they happen.

You can find a copy of "Summer Homework Should Be Banned" in the online resources. Print it out and read it before continuing with this section.

Analyzing "Summer Homework Should Be Banned" for Multiple Teaching Points

Nancy Kalish's "Summer Homework Should Be Banned" (2009) is an argument from *Time for Kids*, a source of great nonfiction mentor texts.

Voice

The use of the dash gives emphasis to the second part of this sentence.

Voice → Single-word or two-word minor sentences give each sentence a dramatic beat.

Focus

The author focuses her argument on the idea that summer isn't the right time for homework. Another way of talking about the focus is that she develops a part of the larger topic of homework.

Structure

The author begins this paragraph with a counter-reason, which she then rebuts with her first reason.

Structure

The author transitions readers from reason to reason by indenting and writing topic sentences.

> Swimming. Softball. Camp. Book reports. It's pretty easy to recognize that one of these things does not belong with the others. Summer is not the right time for homework—and not just because kids hate it. There are some very good reasons why teachers should think twice before piling it on this summer.
>
> Some educators say that doing book reports and math problems help kids retain their skills over the summer. But there's no research proving that kids who don't do summer homework experience long-term learning loss. Chances are, you won't forget how to compute fractions in a few months. You might be rusty in September. But a quick review in class should bring you up to speed. If it doesn't, you might not have been taught the skill well enough.
>
> Summer homework can also take away from the important learning that goes on outside of school . .

Structure

The lead begins with a "which one of these things doesn't belong" hook, followed by the author's claim.

Detail

The author develops a reason with a hypothetical example.

Voice

The author creates a personal tone by using the pronoun *you* to speak directly to the reader.

Detail → The author develops this reason with examples of actions.

> This includes reading for pleasure, which helps you establish a lifelong love of books. Play is also essential. It gives you an opportunity to master social skills, such as teamwork, that will be key to your success as a working adult.
>
> And if you are doing anything that helps you break a sweat, you are also helping your brain develop properly. Research shows that physical exercise is essential to proper brain growth in children. Plus, exercise keeps you healthy.
>
> Finally, it is important to consider how a load of summer homework will make students feel about returning to school. Should kids start the school year feeling burned out and resentful? Or should they return to school refreshed and ready to learn? Shouldn't kids have time to just be kids and not little adults? The answers seem obvious to me. What do you think?

Detail

The author uses transition words to help the reader move from detail to detail.

Detail

↓

The author puts a comma after the dependent clause.

Detail

↓

The author develops this reason by referring to research she's read.

Structure

↓

The author uses transition words to help the reader move from reason to reason.

Structure

↓

The author ends the argument by asking readers what they think.

Reread "Summer Homework Should Be Banned." Where else do you see the author use these crafting techniques? What other ones can you find?

Structure

This argument contains a lead, followed by four sections, each of which develops one of the author's reasons:

Intro
Counter Reason
Reason 1
Reason 2
Reason 3
Reason 4
Ending

Online Resource 4.3
*Guide to Analyzing a
Mentor Text*

How Can You Do This Kind of Analysis Yourself?

You may be amazed by how many craft techniques the authors of *Jabari Jumps*, "Surprising Saturn," and "Summer Homework Should Be Banned" use—and you probably found even more when you reread the texts yourself!

How can you get better at doing this important work, with your own mentor texts, so that you can be prepared for the teaching you'll do with your students? Here are four steps you can take:

1 Do this right away with one of your own mentor texts. Use the "Guide to Analyzing a Mentor Text" form to help you. Record each of your discoveries as you find them on the form.

2 Do this work together with colleagues, using the "Guide to Analyzing a Mentor Text" form to structure the conversation. You'll find that as you analyze a mentor text, each of you will find some different things. This happens because some teachers are more knowledgeable about one quality of writing than about others. Collectively, you'll find many more teaching points than if you do this work by yourself.

3 Build your knowledge base about craft by reading professional books listed on the next page. As you learn more about the qualities of writing, you'll be able to see more teaching points in a mentor text.

4 Analyze mentor texts with your students. (In Chapter 6, you'll learn how to do whole-class text study.) You'll find that your students will often notice ways an author has crafted a text that you or your colleagues haven't noticed before!

Q & A

What books should I have in my craft library?

To help you deepen your knowledge of craft—and be able to see more and more craft techniques in a mentor text—it helps to read professional books on craft.

Two excellent starting points for reading about the craft of writing are Ralph Fletcher's *What a Writer Needs* (2013) and Katie Wood Ray's *Wondrous Words* (1999).

Some professional books contain a variety of craft lessons, such as Ralph Fletcher's *Focus Lessons* (2019), Ralph Fletcher and JoAnn Portalupi's *Craft Lessons* (2007) and *Nonfiction Craft Lessons* (2001a), Lester Laminack's *Cracking Open the Author's Craft* (2016), Jen Serravallo's *The Writing Strategies Book* (2017), and Stacey Shubitz's *Craft Moves* (2016).

Other professional books focus on one aspect of craft. For example, in Barry Lane's *After the End* (2015) and Rozlyn Linder's *The Big Book of Details* (2016), the authors explore how to teach students how to write with detail. Dan Feigelson discusses how to teach students to use punctuation to craft their writing in *Practical Punctuation* (2009). And Katie Wood

Ray talks about illustration study in her book *In Pictures and Words* (2010).

There are many books that discuss the teaching of craft in genre studies. Some of these include Katherine Bomer's *Writing a Life* (memoir) (2005) and *The Journey Is Everything* (essay) (2016); Karen Caine's *Writing to Persuade* (2008); Lucy Calkins and Colleagues' Units of Studies series for grades K–5; M. Colleen Cruz's Writers Read Better series (narrative and nonfiction 2018, 2019); Ralph Fletcher's *Making Nonfiction from Scratch* (2015); Georgia Heard's *For the Good of the Earth and Sun* (1989) and *Awakening the Heart* (poetry) (1999), and *Finding the Heart of Nonfiction* (2013); and Amy Ludwig VanDerwater's *Poems are Teachers* (2018).

Recent books have revisited the qualities of writing through the lens of differing cultural perspectives, a growing body of work that will help us appreciate writing in new, more inclusive ways. Some of these books include Felicia Rose Chavez's *The Anti-Racist Writing Workshop* (2021) and Mathew Salesses' *Craft in the Real World* (2021).

CHAPTER 5

Immerse Students in Mentor Texts

At the beginning of each unit of study in your writing curriculum, familiarize students with the mentor texts you'll be using to teach in that unit. Do this by reading them with your students and also by having students read some themselves. This is called the "immersion" phase of the unit (Ray 2006; Glover and Berry 2012) and it usually lasts for several workshop periods.

Unit of Study Schematic

	Monday	Tuesday	Wednesday	Thursday	Friday
WEEK 1	Immersion			Process lessons on how to choose topics, gather information, make a plan, etc.	
WEEK 2	Process Lessons	Whole-Class Text Study		Craft (and process) lessons while students are drafting and revising.	
WEEK 3	Craft (and process) lessons while students are drafting and revising				
WEEK 4	Conventions lessons while students are editing			Getting ready to publish	Writing celebration

Immersion happens during several days at the beginning of a unit of study.
(Note: Units may be more or less than four weeks long. This is just one way a unit can go.)

Students Should Have an Immersion Experience for Several Reasons:

→ You may find some of the texts you share with students don't interest them. When this happens, consider not using them in the unit, as students won't be as motivated to study and learn from them. Unfortunately, they may sometimes have this reaction to a text that you love, and it may be hard for you to let it go!

Reading mentor texts gets students excited about writing in a unit.

Because you've carefully chosen mentor texts you think students will find relevant and interesting, they will (hopefully) become enthusiastic about the kind of writing they'll be doing in the unit as they read them. If the unit is a genre study, students become eager to write in the genre. Or if the unit is another kind of craft study—for example, an illustration or detail study (Ray 1999; Glover 2019)—students become excited about the focus of the study.

Students start learning about craft when they hear texts read aloud.

As part of immersion, you'll read mentor texts aloud to your students. As they listen, students will pick up a lot of aural information about how the kind of writing you're reading is crafted. Not only do students read like writers, they listen like writers.

Reading mentor texts aloud is especially important for children who are emergent bilinguals, because this helps them become more familiar with the sound and cadence of texts written in English.

Students start learning about craft when they see the texts.

Students first see mentor texts as you read them with them—and they read them themselves—during immersion. Immediately, they start to read like a writer and notice things about the ways that the authors crafted the texts. Although later in the unit you'll lead a whole-class study of one or more of the texts and also use the texts to teach lessons about specific aspects of craft, students will also learn a lot about craft you might not teach explicitly in the unit.

Students start talking about how the texts are crafted.

At the end of immersion, engage your students in their first discussion of how the texts they've read are crafted. By doing this, you've initiated a conversation about craft that will continue throughout the unit.

Q & A *

Should students see the text you're reading aloud?

Yes! When possible, give your students the opportunity to see the text as you read it. This can be as simple as showing students the pages of a picture book as you read it aloud. You can also project the text you're reading using your document camera. And in the upper grades, you can give students printed copies of the text.

Methods for Immersing Students in Mentor Texts

1. The first way to familiarize students with mentor texts is by reading them aloud to your students.

Before you read texts, there is some preparation work to do:

Try to learn about the authors (and illustrators) of the texts so you have some information to share about them when you introduce their texts to students. A quick internet search may turn up the authors' websites or articles about them. You may also be able to find photos of the authors to show your students. Information about authors helps students understand they were written by real people, who had reasons for writing them, that may inspire your students.

Before you read a text, think about how you're going to read it. Is the tone of the text funny? Sad? Angry? Take a couple of minutes to practice reading the text aloud, so you're prepared to read it well.

▷ **Video 5.1**

Immersion in a primary classroom

▷ **Video 5.2**

Immersion in an upper-grade classroom

Just before you read the first text, preview the new unit of study for your students:

If you're beginning a genre study, tell them, "Writers, in our new unit, we're going to be studying a wonderful and interesting kind of nonfiction writing, which is called the feature article. Over the next few days, we're going to be reading several of them so that you get a feel for what this kind of writing is like before you start writing them yourselves."

Or if you're beginning a unit of study that's not a genre study, tell your students what the focus of the unit will be: "Writers, in this new unit, we're going to be studying how writers give their writing voice, that is, the different moves that writers make to give their writing some personality. Over the next few periods, we're going to be reading several texts in different genres in which writers use these moves, moves that you're soon going to be trying yourselves."

→ Use the share screen function on your video conferring platform to make the text you are reading aloud visible to your students.

Then make the reading of each text a dynamic and powerful event:

1

Gather your students together in the classroom meeting area for the read-alouds so that listening to the texts is a communal experience.

2

Read in an animated way. Remember that your enthusiasm for the kind of writing your students will be doing in the unit is contagious.

3

When you are moved by a section of the text, show it! Likewise, when your students have a reaction to a text, pause and give the class a moment to feel its impact.

4

When you finish reading the text, be quiet for a few moments so that your students have time to linger with their responses.

Q & A *

Is it useful to have emergent primary readers meet in partnerships or small groups during immersion?

Absolutely! Students who can't yet read text enjoy looking through the pages of picture books and talking about what they notice and are thinking about the illustrations and text features. And by looking at the pages of a book, they're noticing things about how books are written that they can use when they compose their own.

After you read a text, give your students a chance to respond *as readers* to the *content* of the text. If you've just read a memoir, your students may want to share memories that were sparked by the text. Or if you've just read an all-about non-fiction book, students might want to talk about some of the interesting facts they learned. Remember that when students have had strong responses to a text—and get time to share them and also hear about the ways their classmates have been moved by it—they'll be more interested in studying the craft moves the author used to create these responses.

There are several ways you can choose to have students respond:

Have students share their responses with the class.

Ask students to turn and talk to a classmate about their responses. After a few moments, ask a few students to share their responses with the class.

Have students jot their responses in their writer's notebooks. After giving them a few minutes to do so, ask a few students to share what they wrote with their classmates by turning and talking with a neighboring student, with the whole class, or both.

After reading texts in genres such as op-ed or literary essay, invite students to have a short debate about the authors' opinions or claims in these texts.

However you choose to have students respond to the mentor texts, be sure to name the kinds of responses students are having and to point out that when they write in the unit, their ownbreaders will have the same kinds of responses—because that's how powerful the genre or the aspect of craft they're studying in this unit can be.

2. Another way to immerse students in mentor texts is to have students read some themselves.

Since later in their lives they will have to immerse themselves in writing without any teacher guidance, it's important students have some experience with doing so now, with your support.

Have your students read a text in small groups. One student can read the text aloud to the group, or students can take turns reading it aloud. If there are multiple copies of the text, group members can also decide to read the text to themselves. Once the students have finished reading a text, they share their responses with each other.

Give groups several mentor texts to read. Students can then read through the mentor texts in several ways. For example, they might browse through the mentor texts and decide to read the most enticing one together as a group, and then another one, and so forth, responding to each after they read it. Or after browsing, they could instead read the texts to themselves in whatever order they choose and share their responses when they finish reading.

For older students (grades 2 and above), you can give groups the "Small-Group Immersion Guide: Responding as Readers" sheet to help guide their conversations. [Online Resource 5.2, page 79]

As students are reading texts, your job is to circulate around the room and confer with groups:

> You might need to coach to help groups decide how they're going to read the text(s) or share their responses to the text(s) with each other.

> You could name the kinds of responses you're hearing, and ask if other students had similar ones.

Whole-Class Immersion

1 Read

Read the mentor text aloud in an animated way. When you are moved by a section of the text, show it!

2 Pause

When you finish reading the text, be quiet for a few moments so students can linger with their responses.

3 Respond

Ask students to respond *as readers* to the content of the text by sharing their responses with the class, turning and talking, or by jotting responses in their writers' notebooks and then sharing.

4 Name

As students share, name the kind of responses they're having. Tell students they'll have the same kinds of effects on their readers.

5 Talk about texts like writers

After you finished reading all the mentor texts (which will take several periods), invite students to begin talking about them as writers. Ask them, "What do you notice about the ways the mentor texts are written?"

 Online Resource 5.1
Table Tent: Whole-Class Immersion

A Teacher's Guide to Mentor Texts

End Immersion by Nudging Students to Respond to the Mentor Texts as Writers

At the end of the immersion phase of a unit, invite students to discuss their first impressions of how the mentor texts are written. This shift initiates a conversation about what students are learning from the texts as writers, a conversation that will continue throughout the rest of the unit in deeper and deeper ways.

1. The first way you can invite your students to talk about the mentor texts as writers is in a whole-class discussion.

This will help students feel they're part of a shared inquiry about the kind of writing or craft they're studying in the unit from the get-go. And they'll learn from each other as they share their observations.

Ask your students to gather in the meeting area.	**Begin the discussion by asking students what they've been noticing about the way the mentor texts have been written. If the unit is a genre study, you might say, "Writers, now that we've read several how-to books, what have you been noticing about the way this kind of writing goes?" If the unit focuses on an aspect of craft, you might say, "Writers, what have you been noticing so far about the ways that writers use detail in their writing?"**	**As students share their observations, write them down on chart paper or on a piece of paper that you're projecting with a document camera.**

continues on next page

Two charts: one in which the teacher recorded students' observations about a genre, and another in which the teachers recorded students' observations about an aspect of craft:

continued from previous page

If students share responses to the content of the mentor texts—"The stories are really exciting" or "The opinion pieces sometimes made me feel angry"—redirect them by saying, "What did the writers of the texts do *as writers* to make you feel this way?"

Keep in mind that the students are sharing their first impressions of the kind of writing or craft they're studying, which may not be very sophisticated! As the unit progresses, their observations will become more precise in response to further study and teaching. Also, as your students talk in unit after unit about how texts are crafted, the level of their conversations will improve.

FEATURE ARTICLES

- Lots of facts
- Fun titles
- Divided into sections
- Some sections have illustrations
- Lots of different text features (diagrams, fun facts, definition boxes)
- Fun comparisons
- Lots of adjectives to describe things
- Catchy subheadings
- Authors sometimes make jokes
- Interesting ledes

ILLUSTRATION STUDY
WHAT WE NOTICE ILLUSTRATORS DO

- Use lots of colors in illustrations
- "Zoom in" in a picture
- Put labels on parts of an illustration
- Put motion lines by a character
- Include several illustration panels on a page
- "Zoom out" and show everything
- Show characters from behind, side, front
- Put "fun facts" in an illustration
- Facial expressions show characters' feelings
- Dialogue and thought bubbles
- Background details

2. You can also have students respond to the mentor texts as writers in small groups, which has several advantages.

Students who are reluctant to share their observations with the whole class may feel more comfortable when they're talking with just a few classmates. You'll be able to circulate from group to group and coach students as they try to talk about the mentor texts as writers. The conversations students have in small groups helps to prepare them for whole-class discussions.

Before the small groups meet, tell your class you would like them to discuss what students have been noticing about the genre they've been reading or what they've been noticing about the aspect of craft they're studying in the unit. For older students (grades 2 and above), you can give groups the "Small-Group Immersion Guide: Responding as Writers" sheet to help guide their conversations. [Online Resource 5.3]

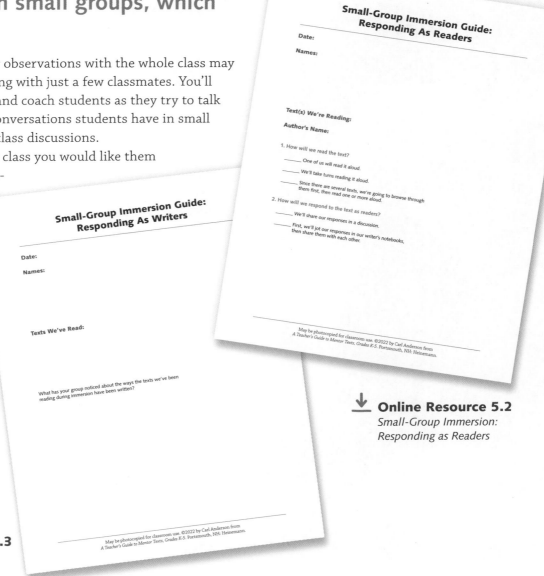

Small-Group Immersion Guide: Responding As Readers

Date:

Names:

Text(s) We're Reading:

Author's Name:

1. How will we read the text?

_____ One of us will read it aloud.

_____ We'll take turns reading it aloud.

_____ Since there are several texts, we're going to browse through them first, then read one or more aloud.

2. How will we respond to the text as readers?

_____ We'll share our responses in a discussion.

_____ First, we'll jot our responses in our writer's notebooks, then share them with each other.

May be photocopied for classroom use. ©2022 by Carl Anderson from
A Teacher's Guide to Mentor Texts, Grades K–5. Portsmouth, NH: Heinemann.

Small-Group Immersion Guide: Responding As Writers

Date:

Names:

Texts We've Read:

What has your group noticed about the ways the texts we've been reading during immersion have been written?

May be photocopied for classroom use. ©2022 by Carl Anderson from
A Teacher's Guide to Mentor Texts, Grades K–5. Portsmouth, NH: Heinemann.

⬇ **Online Resource 5.2**
Small-Group Immersion: Responding as Readers

⬇ **Online Resource 5.3**
Small-Group Immersion: Responding as Writers

Planning the Immersion Phase of a Unit

When you're planning the immersion part of a unit, you first need to decide how many days to devote to it. Generally, 2–4 days of immersion will give students the opportunity to read and discuss enough texts and get a sense of the kind of writing they'll be doing in the unit. You'll find that if the unit focuses on a kind of writing or craft that is new to your students or will be challenging for them, you'll want to give more time to immersion.

You also need to decide how to structure each day of immersion. These days do **not** follow the typical structure of writing workshop of a mini-lesson followed by independent writing and a share session. Think about the ways you'll immerse students in the mentor texts each day, as well as how you'll have them respond. It's a good idea to do whole-class read-alouds on the first day, so that your students have a shared experience with reading and responding to the texts. On subsequent days, give your students some opportunities to read and respond in small groups, so they have some independent experiences with immersion.

The following sample immersion plan is designed for three days. This is just one of many ways immersion could go! You might choose to do two or four days and do a different combination of immersion experiences each day.

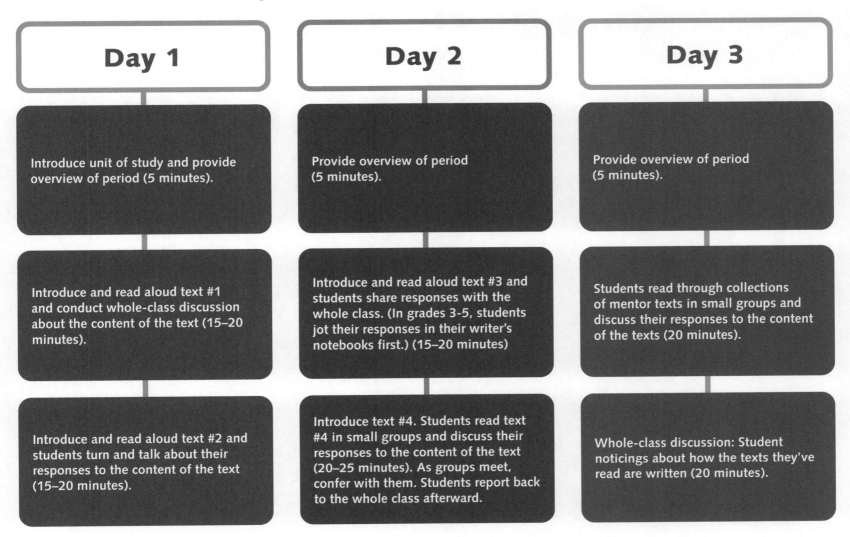

Day 1

Introduce unit of study and provide overview of period (5 minutes).

Introduce and read aloud text #1 and conduct whole-class discussion about the content of the text (15–20 minutes).

Introduce and read aloud text #2 and students turn and talk about their responses to the content of the text (15–20 minutes).

Day 2

Provide overview of period (5 minutes).

Introduce and read aloud text #3 and students share responses with the whole class. (In grades 3-5, students jot their responses in their writer's notebooks first.) (15–20 minutes)

Introduce text #4. Students read text #4 in small groups and discuss their responses to the content of the text (20–25 minutes). As groups meet, confer with them. Students report back to the whole class afterward.

Day 3

Provide overview of period (5 minutes).

Students read through collections of mentor texts in small groups and discuss their responses to the content of the texts (20 minutes).

Whole-class discussion: Student noticings about how the texts they've read are written (20 minutes).

STEP 4

Lead Whole-Class Text Study

> This chapter has its roots in Katie Wood Ray's foundational work on the teaching of craft that she writes about in her book, *Wondrous Words* (1999).

When you're doing a unit of study that focuses on the craft of writing, one of the most important parts of the unit is *whole-class text study*. To do this, lead your class through an extended discussion and analysis of one or more of your class mentor texts.

You'll do whole-class text study for several reasons:

- These conversations help create a community of writers in your classroom who study the craft of writing together.

- Students get a guided experience with reading like a writer.

- Students get the experience of constructing craft knowledge themselves, instead of relying on teachers to do so for them.

- Students learn about studying craft from each other as they hear what classmates notice and have to say about texts.

- Students build a class repertoire of craft techniques they can try in their writing.

- Students' enthusiasm for trying new craft techniques is greater when they feel they've discovered these techniques themselves.

- You learn about what kinds of craft techniques are interesting to your students, which can then become the focus of mini-lessons, small groups, and conferences.

Units of Study that Focus on Craft

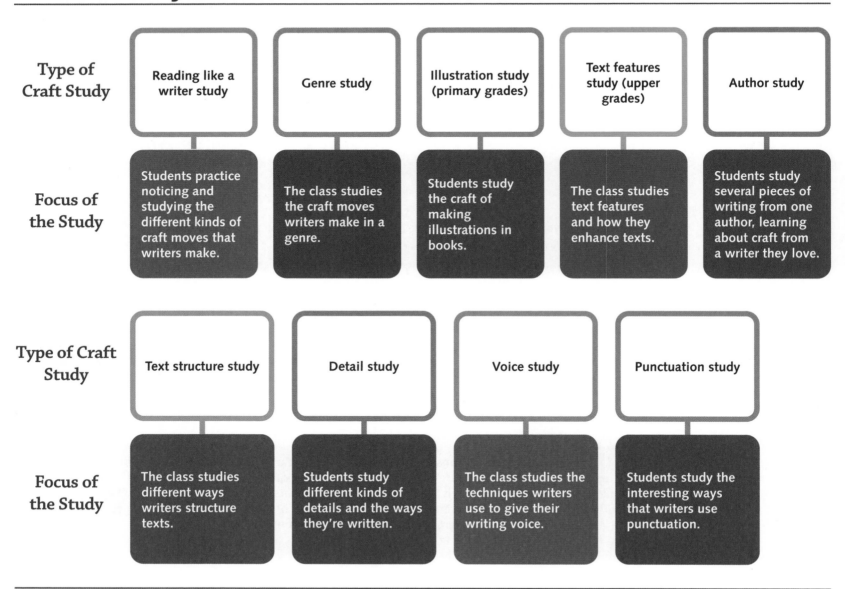

Type of Craft Study	Reading like a writer study	Genre study	Illustration study (primary grades)	Text features study (upper grades)	Author study
Focus of the Study	Students practice noticing and studying the different kinds of craft moves that writers make.	The class studies the craft moves writers make in a genre.	Students study the craft of making illustrations in books.	The class studies text features and how they enhance texts.	Students study several pieces of writing from one author, learning about craft from a writer they love.

Type of Craft Study	Text structure study	Detail study	Voice study	Punctuation study
Focus of the Study	The class studies different ways writers structure texts.	Students study different kinds of details and the ways they're written.	The class studies the techniques writers use to give their writing voice.	Students study the interesting ways that writers use punctuation.

A Teacher's Guide to Mentor Texts

How to Do Whole-Class Text Study: Five Steps

The best time to do a whole-class text study in a unit is after you've taught your students what they need to learn about the rehearsal stage of the writing process—finding topics, gathering information for drafts—and many of your students are either ready to draft or have begun drafts.

In this unit of study, whole-class text study occurs for two days, once the students have begun to work on drafts. (Note: The days could have also been scheduled deeper into the time that students are drafting and revising. The days could also be spread out.)

Unit of Study Schematic

	Monday	Tuesday	Wednesday	Thursday	Friday
WEEK 1	Immersion			Process lessons on how to choose topics, gather information, make a plan, etc.	
WEEK 2	Process Lessons	Whole-Class Text Study		Craft (and process) lessons while students are drafting and revising.	
WEEK 3	Craft (and process) lessons while students are drafting and revising				
WEEK 4	Conventions lessons while students are editing			Getting ready to publish	Writing celebration

Q&A ✳

Where can I learn about how to do craft studies?

You can learn about how to do many kinds of craft studies in books such as Matt Glover's *Craft and Process Studies* (2019) and Katie Wood Ray's *Study Driven* (2006). Dan Feigelson's *Practical Punctuation* (2009) and Katie Wood Ray's *In Pictures and Words* (illustration study) (2010) describe how to do a study of one aspect of craft. There are many books on teaching genre studies, including Katherine Bomer's *Writing a Life* (2005) and *The Journey Is Everything* (essay) (2016), Karen Caine's *Writing to Persuade* (2008), Ralph Fletcher's *Making Nonfiction from Scratch* (2015), M. Colleen Cruz's Writers Read Better series (narrative and nonfiction 2018, 2019), Georgia Heard's *For the Good of the Earth and Sun* (1989) and *Awakening the Heart* (poetry) (1999), and *Finding the Heart of Nonfiction* (2013), and Chris Lehman's *Energize Research Reading and Writing* (2012).

When you do a whole-class text study, you'll suspend the normal structure of writing workshop that day (mini-lesson, independent writing, share session). Instead, you and your class will have a discussion about a mentor text that may last anywhere from fifteen minutes to the entire period depending upon the grade you teach, students' experience with this kind of study, and their enthusiasm for studying the text. (If the study goes on for less than a period, then have students write independently for the remainder of the time.)

In some units of study, you may just have time for one whole-class text study. In others, you might devote several periods to the study of one mentor text, or several. Of course, the more time you're able to devote to whole-class study, the more guided experience with reading like a writer your students will gain and the larger the repertoire of craft techniques they'll discover.

▷ **Video 6.1**

Whole-Class Text Study in a Primary Classroom

▷ **Video 6.2**

Whole-Class Text Study in an Upper-Grade Classroom

• WORDS FROM TEACHER MENTORS •

"By engaging students in the definition process, you confirm that knowledge construction is fluid—that there are multiple interpretations of the 'right' way to write—while simultaneously empowering students to claim ownership of their artistic community."

Felicia Rose Chavez (2021)

When you lead a whole-class text study, follow these five steps:

Step 1: Reread the mentor text.

Begin the study by bringing your class together and telling the students they'll be doing one of the most important things that writers do to get better at writing, which is to study a mentor text to see what writers do to write well, and then try out what they learn in their own writing. Tell them this period will go differently than other writing workshop periods because they'll be studying the mentor text for half the period, maybe even the whole period.

If this is the first time your class is doing whole-class text study, you might describe experiences they've had in which they've done a similar kind of study. For example, you might talk about how children who play sports often watch more experienced athletes in person or on television, notice the moves these athletes make, and then try the moves out themselves.

When possible, before you start, give your students copies of the mentor text, so they can write on it. If that's not possible—for example, if you're studying a picture book with your class—then as you read the text, project the pages onto a screen or SMART Board using your document camera.

→ **You can post a copy of the text on Google Classroom for your students to print out before you do a whole-class text study with them.**

→ **Use the share screen function on your video conferring platform to make the text you are rereading visible to your students.**

• **WORDS FROM TEACHER MENTORS** •

> *"When students are taught to see how writing is done, this way of seeing opens up for them huge warehouses of possibilities for how to make their writing **good** writing."*

Katie Wood Ray (1999)

Q & A ✳

Which mentor text(s) should my class study?

By the end of the immersion phase, you will have read several mentor texts to your class. Choose a text for whole-class text study that your class especially enjoyed reading that is full of craft techniques you think your students will be able to notice, and ultimately use, in their writing.

Next, explain to your students that you're going to reread a mentor text and as you're reading, they'll look for parts of the texts that make them say, "I like the way the author wrote that!".

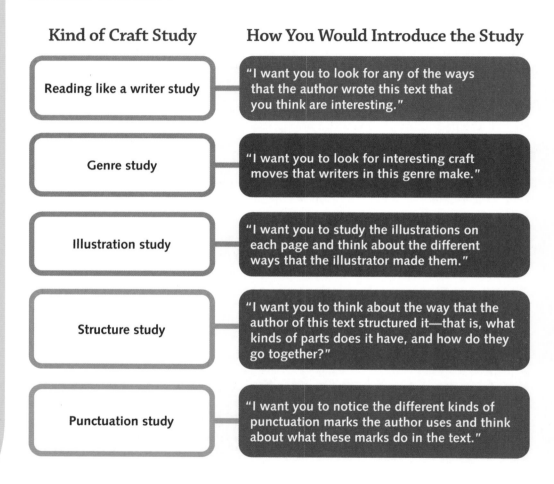

Kind of Craft Study	How You Would Introduce the Study
Reading like a writer study	"I want you to look for any of the ways that the author wrote this text that you think are interesting."
Genre study	"I want you to look for interesting craft moves that writers in this genre make."
Illustration study	"I want you to study the illustrations on each page and think about the different ways that the illustrator made them."
Structure study	"I want you to think about the way that the author of this text structured it—that is, what kinds of parts does it have, and how do they go together?"
Punctuation study	"I want you to notice the different kinds of punctuation marks the author uses and think about what these marks do in the text."

Then reread the text. Just as you did during immersion, read the text in an animated way. If students have a copy of the text, they should use their pencil or marker to put a check next to parts they like or underline or circle parts that stand out to them.

Step 2: Students share what they noticed.

After you're done rereading the text, have students read their favorite parts aloud. You can do this very simply, by asking students to raise their hands to let you know they want to share. If they have a copy of the mentor text, they'll read from it. If they don't, they'll tell you which part of the text they want you to zoom in on with the document camera so they can read it.

You can also do what Katie Wood Ray (1999) calls a *symphony share*, in which students are in charge of the sharing. One student begins reading, and as soon as they finish reading, another chimes in—without having to raise their hand to be called on—and so on.

Have students share for several minutes. Note on your copy of the mentor text which parts the students read, as you'll soon be discussing some of them.

→ As students read their favorite parts aloud, use the annotation function on your video conferencing platform to underline or circle these parts.

Step 3: Select which parts to discuss.

Once students have shared their favorite parts, decide which ones to discuss as a class. Decide to talk about a part when any of the following occur:

It's obvious many students liked it. You'll know this when a student reads a part, and the class "oohs" and "aahs," or you hear them whisper that they liked that part, too. Sometimes, several students will read the same part—more evidence it's a popular one.

Some of the parts students read are craft techniques you think students will be more successful discussing and trying out in their writing. This will be an especially important consideration when your class is new to whole-class text study.

One of students' favorite parts contains a craft technique you want students to learn in this unit of study.

Step 4: Discuss several craft techniques.

The discussion part of the study is the most important part. Invite your students to read like writers, and give them the support they need to be successful.

Craft Techniques

1

First, read the selected part aloud.

"Next playgroup, I have a new bathing suit. It is just like Tamika's—two piece, with pink butterflies and three rows of ruffles." (From *My Best Friend*, by Mary Ann Rodman [2005])

2

Ask the class, "What do you notice about how the writer wrote this part?"

Student: She describes Lily's bathing suit with a lot of words.

Teacher: A lot of words . . . say more about that.

Student: She makes a list of things about the bathing suit.

Teacher: A list of things . . . what exactly do you see the author doing in this sentence?

Student: There are three things in the list.

Student: And there are commas in between the things on the list.

Student: And there's a line thingy before the list!

Student: That's called a dash.

3

Ask the class, "Why do you think the author used this craft technique?"

Student: The author wants us to be able to see how pretty Lily's bathing suit is . . .

Student: Yes, she wants us to make a picture in our heads about the bathing suit.

Teacher: So you're saying this craft technique helps us see in our heads what the author is writing about.

4

Ask the class, "What name do you want to give this craft technique?"

Student: Let's call this . . . a "Description List!"

Students: Ooh . . . That's a good name.

5

Ask the class, "Have we seen other authors use this crafting technique?"

Student: I think I remember one in *Jabari Jumps*, in the part that describes the diving board.

Teacher: Why don't you go look, and share that part with us later?

There are several predictable difficulties students will have in the discussion part of the study:

 Students respond as readers, not writers, to a part of the text.

When students are new to whole-class text study, they'll often respond in readerly ways. When this happens, guide your students toward describing what the writer is actually *doing* in the text. The more precisely students describe a craft technique, the better they'll be able to envision using the craft technique themselves.

Here's how to reply when students respond as readers:

→ If your students are new to whole-class text study, it's a good idea to model what it means to talk about a part as a writer by selecting a part you like, and then describing what you notice the writer did in that part.

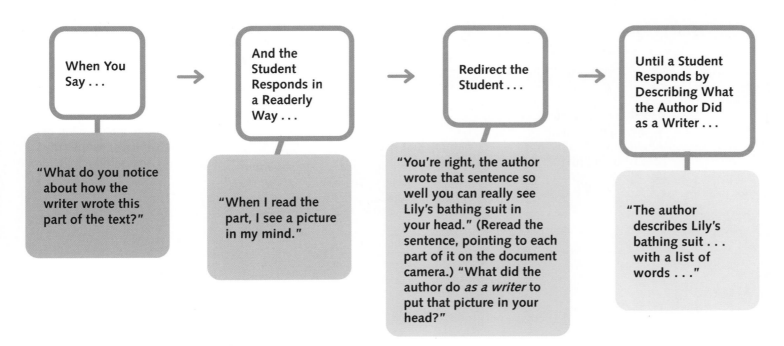

When You Say . . .

"What do you notice about how the writer wrote this part of the text?"

→ **And the Student Responds in a Readerly Way . . .**

"When I read the part, I see a picture in my mind."

→ **Redirect the Student . . .**

"You're right, the author wrote that sentence so well you can really see Lily's bathing suit in your head." (Reread the sentence, pointing to each part of it on the document camera.) "What did the author do *as a writer* to put that picture in your head?"

→ **Until a Student Responds by Describing What the Author Did as a Writer . . .**

"The author describes Lily's bathing suit . . . with a list of words . . ."

② Students describe the craft technique in a general way.

Students' initial attempts to describe crafting techniques are sometimes imprecise, even when they are experienced at reading like a writer. Students will often need to make multiple attempts at describing a technique, building on what each other says until they're successful.

Here's how to respond to your class to help them describe craft moves more precisely.

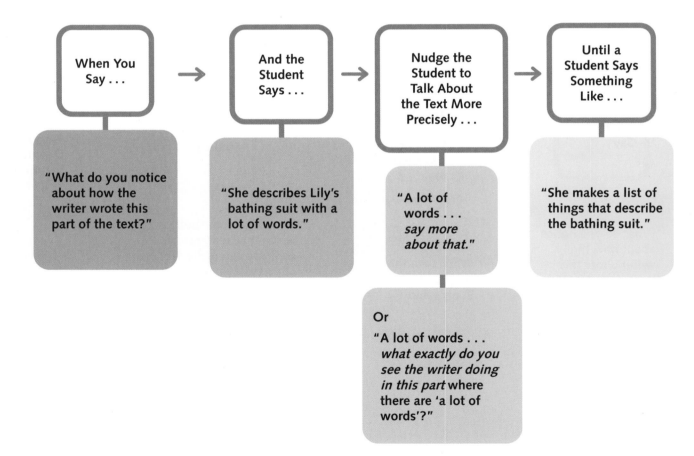

When You Say . . .	And the Student Says . . .	Nudge the Student to Talk About the Text More Precisely . . .	Until a Student Says Something Like . . .
"What do you notice about how the writer wrote this part of the text?"	"She describes Lily's bathing suit with a lot of words."	"A lot of words . . . *say more about that.*" **Or** "A lot of words . . . *what exactly do you see the writer doing in this part* where there are 'a lot of words'?"	"She makes a list of things that describe the bathing suit."

③ Students are unsure about why the author used the craft technique.

In reality, we don't really know why authors use many craft techniques. The point of asking students this question is to have them speculate about the purposes for using craft techniques, so they can imagine reasons why they can use these techniques themselves.

One way to help students speculate is to ask them about the effects the craft techniques have on them as readers. It may take your students several tries to get somewhere, and it's possible they may come up with several valid theories about why the author used a technique.

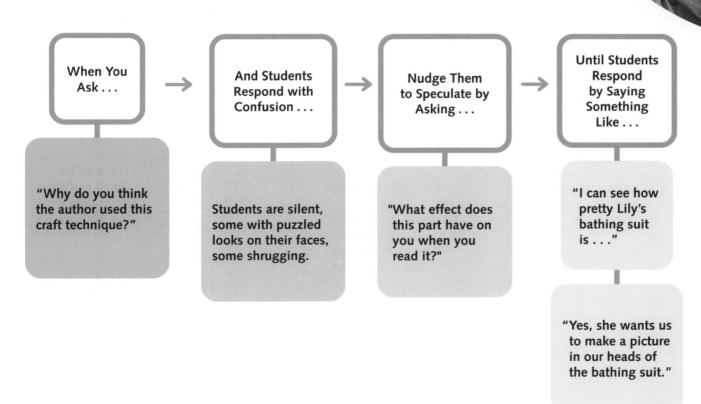

When You Ask . . .

"Why do you think the author used this craft technique?"

→

And Students Respond with Confusion . . .

Students are silent, some with puzzled looks on their faces, some shrugging.

→

Nudge Them to Speculate by Asking . . .

"What effect does this part have on you when you read it?"

→

Until Students Respond by Saying Something Like . . .

"I can see how pretty Lily's bathing suit is . . ."

"Yes, she wants us to make a picture in our heads of the bathing suit."

④ Students give craft techniques generic names.

Asking students to come up with names for the craft techniques they discuss creates a shared language you and your students can use when you talk about these techniques during the unit of study and beyond. It's important your students come up with precise names for craft techniques that help them imagine what to do when they use the techniques themselves.

Students often come up with generic names for craft techniques. When they do, nudge them toward more specificity:

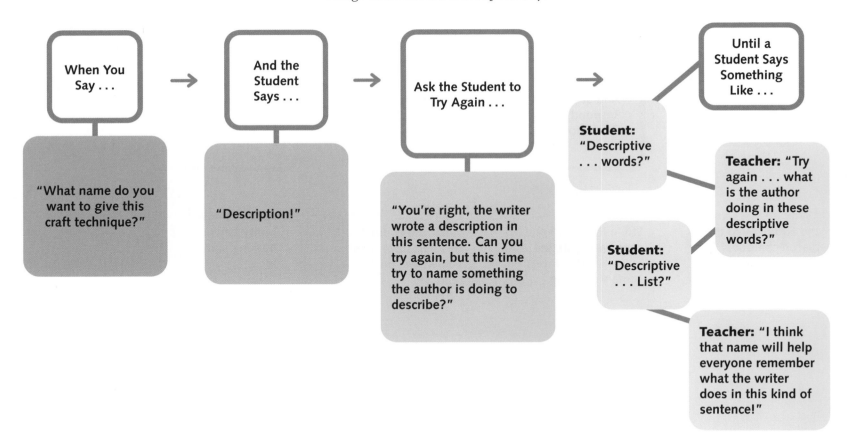

When You Say . . .

"What name do you want to give this craft technique?"

→

And the Student Says . . .

"Description!"

→

Ask the Student to Try Again . . .

"You're right, the writer wrote a description in this sentence. Can you try again, but this time try to name something the author is doing to describe?"

→

Until a Student Says Something Like . . .

Student: "Descriptive . . . words?"

Teacher: "Try again . . . what is the author doing in these descriptive words?"

Student: "Descriptive . . . List?"

Teacher: "I think that name will help everyone remember what the writer does in this kind of sentence!"

As part of Step 4, chart what students say about the craft techniques they discuss. (This chart is based on one from Katie Wood Ray's *Wondrous Words* [1999]). Notice in the chart that there's an additional column where students can write an example of how they tried the craft technique in their writing. Students can also write their examples on sticky notes and then place them in this column.

Photo of chart from a classroom.

↓ **Online Resource 6.1**
Whole-Class Text Study Chart

Step 5: Invite students to try out the craft techniques.

The ultimate point of whole-class text inquiry is for students to try out the craft techniques they discover in their own writing and build their own craft repertoires. There are several ways of encouraging them to "have a go" with the techniques you discuss with them:

(1) **If there is still some time left in the period for students to write after whole-class craft study, ask students to commit to trying at least one of the techniques in their writing that day.**

(2) **On the day after you've done a study, give a mini-lesson in which you demonstrate how to try a craft technique your students discussed in the study:**

Good to see you today, writers! Spending time studying Mary Ann Rodman's *My Best Friend* has been really exciting. You did a great job noticing and discussing some of the craft techniques she used in the story.

Because I'm hoping that you'll try out some of the craft techniques Mary Ann Rodman used in your own writing, today I'm going to show you how you can do this. I'm going to try out one of the techniques—the "Description List"—in my own writing.

I thought I would try this one out because in the story I'm writing about walking through the park that's near where I live in Brooklyn, I want to create a picture in readers' minds of the lake I walked by, just like we can see Lily's bathing suit in our minds when we read *My Best Friend*. I'm up to this part in my story:

> *After walking past the ball fields, the lake appeared on my left.*

I really want to describe what the lake looks like, and I think Mary Ann Rodman can help me. First, I'm going to reread the "Description List" to remind myself how she wrote the description. (I read out loud, "Next playgroup, I have a new bathing suit. It is just like Tamika's two piece, with pink butterflies and three rows of ruffles.") Rereading this, I'm reminded that she names what she's going to describe—Tamika's bathing suit—and then lists several phrases that describe what it looks like.

I want to describe what the lake looks like, so I need to think about several phrases that describe it, just like Mary Ann Rodman. Hmm . . . the lake is called Prospect Park Lake . . . well, it's big and round . . . sunlight was sparkling on the surface of the water . . . and there were swans swimming near the shore. I think I've got it! (I write.)

> *After walking past the ball fields, the Prospect Park Lake appeared on my left—it was big and round, with sunlight sparkling on the surface, and swans swimming near the shore.*

So you can try out any of the craft techniques you want in your writing, just like I did. Think about what you want to do in your writing, and which technique will help you do it. Then reread the example to remind yourself of what the author did. And then give it a try!

Before you go back to your table to write, would you look at the class chart of craft techniques and think about which ones you might want to try today. (I give the students a moment to look at the chart and choose.)

Thumbs up if there's at least one craft technique you're planning on trying today. (Most students give a thumbs up.) Great. Off you go!

Q & A ✳

What if the unit of study guide I'm using doesn't include whole-class text study?

You can easily insert a whole-class text study into a unit of study! Look for a place in the unit in which students are getting ready to draft or are already drafting. You'll find adding one or several periods of study will help your students become more enthusiastic about craft, because they'll feel more ownership of the craft techniques they discover themselves.

3 In share sessions, spotlight students who try out craft techniques the class discussed in the study.

4 Give students a copy of the chart of craft techniques to put in their folders, so they can refer to it easily when they want to try a technique in their writing.

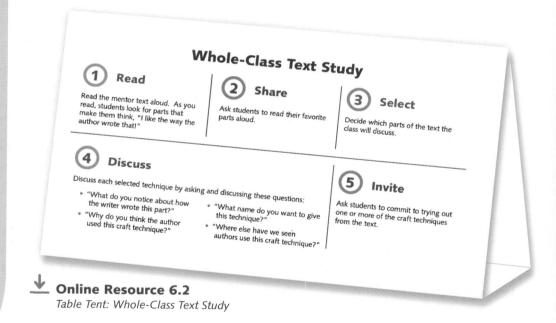

Whole-Class Text Study

1 Read

Read the mentor text aloud. As you read, students look for parts that make them think, "I like the way the author wrote that!"

2 Share

Ask students to read their favorite parts aloud.

3 Select

Decide which parts of the text the class will discuss.

4 Discuss

Discuss each selected technique by asking and discussing these questions:
- "What do you notice about how the writer wrote this part?"
- "Why do you think the author used this craft technique?"
- "What name do you want to give this technique?"
- "Where else have we seen authors use this craft technique?"

5 Invite

Ask students to commit to trying out one or more of the craft techniques from the text.

↓ **Online Resource 6.2**
Table Tent: Whole-Class Text Study

A Teacher's Guide to Mentor Texts

After you've done whole-class text study in several units, try having students do this in small groups instead. As students annotate and discuss a mentor text, confer with each group and help students get even better at reading like writers. Students can record their notic-ings and thinking on their own copy of the "Whole-Class Text Study Chart" (in the online resources).

STEP 5 Teach with Mentor Texts

se mentor texts to teach in craft and conventions lessons, which you'll
give when students are drafting, revising, and editing:

Unit of Study Schematic

	Monday	Tuesday	Wednesday	Thursday	Friday
WEEK 1	Immersion			Process lessons on how to choose topics, gather information, make a plan, etc.	
WEEK 2	Process Lessons	Whole-Class Text Study		Craft (and process) lessons while students are drafting and revising	
WEEK 3	Craft (and process) lessons while students are drafting and revising				
WEEK 4	Conventions lessons while students are editing			Getting ready to publish	Writing celebration

You may feel daunted when you try to read like a writer and describe precisely what writers do when they use a craft move or convention, which you need to do to give a good direct instruction lesson. This isn't surprising, since you probably didn't get much experience with reading like a writer in school yourself! You may also feel this way when you teach a craft technique for the first time, even if you feel confident describing other craft techniques or conventions you've taught before.

To describe a craft move or convention precisely, reread the excerpt of the text that contains it, and ask yourself, "What exactly do I see the writer doing here?" Then try to describe what you see as best you can. You may need to reread the text several times as you think about how to describe what the writer is doing.

As you teach the craft move or convention again and again, you'll find you get better and better at describing it! You'll also get better by discussing mentor texts with colleagues, and hearing how they talk about them.

You'll teach several kinds of lessons:

1 *Mini-lessons,* the whole-class lessons that begin writing workshop most days

2 *Small-group lessons* for 3–5 students during independent writing time

3 *Writing conferences,* one-on-one conversations about their writing with students, also during independent writing time

Two Types of Lessons

1. Direct Instruction

In this type of lesson, it's your job to describe the craft technique or convention you're teaching, using these teaching moves:

1 Name what you're teaching.	**2** Explain its importance.	**3** Show an example of the craft technique or convention in a mentor text, naming the author.
4 Read the example aloud.	**5** Describe how the author uses the technique or convention.	**6** Explain a strategy students can use to try out the technique or convention.

Look for these direct instruction moves in the following lesson:

1. Name the craft technique you're teaching.

Today I want to talk about how you can write the parts, or scenes, of your stories better by mixing character actions, thoughts, and dialogue together as you write them.

2. Explain why the craft technique is important to learn.

Doing this will help readers get a clearer picture of what's happening in the scene.

3. Show the mentor text, naming the author.

Let's take a look at how Gaia Cornwall weaves these kinds of details together in *Jabari Jumps*:

(Reads aloud.)

Jabari started to climb. Up and up.
This ladder is very tall, he thought.
"Are you okay?" called his dad.
"I'm just a little tired," said Jabari.
"Maybe you should climb down and take a tiny rest," said his dad.
A tiny rest sounded like a good idea.

4. Read aloud the excerpt of the text containing the technique.

5. Then, describe how the author used the craft technique as precisely as you can, using your skill with reading like a writer.

I noticed when Gaia Cornwall wrote this scene, she started by describing one of Jabari's actions, that is, what he was doing with his body: "Jabari started to climb. Up and up." *(The teacher points to the line while reading it aloud.)* Right after this action, Gaia tells us what Jabari is thinking *(points to the line)*, "This ladder is very tall, he thought." Then she writes another kind of detail, this time a dialogue between Jabari's dad and Jabari *(reads the three lines of dialogue beginning with, "Are you okay . . .")*. Finally, Gaia ends this part with another one of Jabari's thoughts, "A tiny rest sounded like a good idea."

So Gaia Cornwall writes three kinds of details in this scene—action, thinking, and dialogue—and mixes them together. By doing this, she helps readers see and hear what was happening in this part of the story, and also gets us into Jabari's mind, so we know how he was experiencing what was happening.

How can you do this? When you start each part of your story, ask yourself, "Do I want to start by telling what a character is doing? Thinking? Or maybe with some dialogue?" Then, after you write each detail, keep asking yourself the same questions. As you come up with answers to these questions, add these new details into your drafts.

6. Finally, explain a strategy that students can use to try the craft technique themselves.

2. Inquiry

In this type of lesson, you put the students in the driver's seat by asking them to "read like writers" and study a craft technique or convention, with your guidance. You have two goals in this type of lesson: first, that students learn about the technique or convention and, second, that they get practice with reading like writers.

You'll make these teaching move in an inquiry lesson:

1 Name the aspect of craft or conventions students will be studying.

2 Show an example of the craft technique or convention in a mentor text, naming the author.

3 Cue the students that this will be an inquiry lesson, and read the text aloud.

4 Ask, "What do you notice about what the writer/illustrator did in this part?"

5 Support the student(s) as they try to read like a writer, as necessary.

6 Ask, "Why do you think the writer used this craft technique?"

7 Suggest that students give the craft technique a name.

8 Explain a strategy students can use to try out the technique or convention.

Look for these teaching moves in the following lesson:

1. Name the aspect of craft your students will be studying.

Today I want to talk about the interesting lead.

2. Show the text, and name the author.

Nancy Kalish wrote for her argument, "Summer Homework Should Be Banned." When we first read this piece, I could tell this lead drew everyone into the piece immediately! So I think you'll be interested in learning about the moves she made

in writing the lead, so you can try them yourself.

To study this lead, I'm going to read it aloud, and as I do, I want you to notice what Nancy does *as a writer* in it. Then we'll discuss all the things you notice.

(Reads aloud the first paragraph [see page X]). NOTE: The lead is currently on

3. Cue students this is going to be an inquiry lesson and read the excerpt of the text aloud.

A Teacher's Guide to Mentor Texts

page 62 in manuscript)

4. Ask what the student(s) notice about how the text is written.

So, what did you notice about what Nancy Kalish did as a writer in this lead?

Student: She started with a list.

That's a good noticing.

Say more about that.

5. Support the student(s) as they try to read like a writer.

Student: The last thing in the list—book reports—doesn't belong with the others. She even tells us that in the next sentence!

That's an interesting noticing.

Why do you think she did this?

6. Ask why the author used the craft technique.

Student: Well it surprised me when she said "book reports," just like it surprises me when teachers say we're going to have homework over the summer . . . so this last thing on this list gets readers thinking about what the piece is going to be about.

What else do you notice Nancy Kalish does in the lead, like in the sentence "Summer is not the right time for homework—and not just because kids hate it."

Student: That's her opinion, her claim.

So you're noticing after starting with the list, she tells her opinion. What about the last sentence?

Student: Well, she tells us she's got some reasons. But she doesn't tell us what they are!

Why do you think she does that?

Student: She's going to tell us her reasons in the rest of the piece, so maybe she's creating a little suspense this way?

Interesting theory.

So does anyone have an idea of what we can call this kind of lead?

Student: It's a "Start with a List lead"?

Student: Or it's a "Start with a List Where One Thing Doesn't Belong lead." *(Other students give a thumbs up.)*

Great ideas for naming this lead!

7. Ask the students to give the craft technique a name.

So, to write a lead like this yourself, it seems you'll need to think of something that is kind of opposite to what you're writing about—for example, if you were writing about playground bullying, your list might start with "playing tag," "jumping rope," and "playing catch," which are the usual things kids do on the playground, right? Then you need to come up with something that doesn't belong in that list that connects to your opinion—I guess I could end my list with "being called names." After you do that, writing the rest of the lead seems pretty straightforward—like Nancy, you could write your opinion, then let readers know you'll be explaining the reasons for it.

8. Explain a strategy students can use to try the craft technique themselves.

How do you decide to do an inquiry lesson?

If your students are new to studying craft, it's best to do an inquiry mini-lesson with craft techniques that are visually obvious, such as those that involve the ways text is written; for example, bold words, italics, or the ways words are written on the page (of course, punctuation is very visual, and lends itself well to inquiry lessons), or those that are dramatic and high interest (such as the lead in this sample lesson). As students become more experienced with craft study, have them study more sophisticated craft techniques that aren't as obvious.

Mini-Lessons

Writing workshop usually begins with a mini-lesson (unless you're doing immersion or a whole-class text study that day). Mini-lessons are typically 10–12 minutes long.

There are several reasons you'll teach your class about specific craft techniques and conventions in mini-lessons:

The next lesson in your unit of study guide or the unit you projected is a craft or convention lesson.	As you talk to students in writing conferences, and as you read through their writing, you'll notice many students have a need to learn about a technique or convention.	You've noticed students are excited about a craft technique or convention they've noticed during the immersion phase of the unit, or when you've done whole-class study of a mentor text.

▷ **Video 7.1**

Direction instruction mini-lesson —primary grades

▷ **Video 7.2**

Inquiry mini-lesson—primary grades

▷ **Video 7.3**

Direct instruction mini-lesson —upper grades

▷ **Video 7.4**

Inquiry instruction mini-lesson —upper grades

Mini-lessons have four parts (Anderson 2000; Calkins 1994; Eickholdt and Vitale-Reilly 2022):

① The *connection*, in which you explain why you're teaching the lesson.

② The *teaching point*, in which you teach students about one aspect of writing. In a craft or conventions lesson, this is where you'll show students mentor texts, and you'll teach either by direct instruction or inquiry.

③ The *try-it*, where the students have a go for a few minutes with what you just taught.

④ The *link*, when you set an expectation that many students will try the mini-lesson as they write today.

Lesson Prep:
MINI-LESSONS

- You need a copy of the mentor text(s) you plan to show students during the lesson. You might simply show students pages from a picture book, or project the text using a document camera.

- If you're planning on annotating the mentor text(s) during the lesson, you'll need an annotation tool, such as a pencil or marker if you're projecting the text using a document camera, or the annotation functions on the SMART Board.

- Students need a copy of their current draft of their writing for the try-it part of the mini-lesson and a pen or pencil.

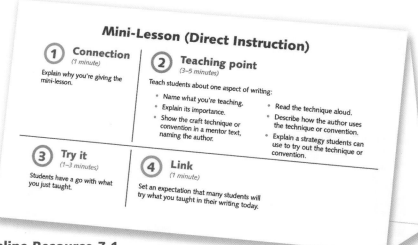

Mini-Lesson (Direct Instruction)

① Connection
(1 minute)
Explain why you're giving the mini-lesson.

② Teaching point
(3–5 minutes)
Teach students about one aspect of writing:
- Name what you're teaching.
- Explain its importance.
- Show the craft technique or convention in a mentor text, naming the author.
- Read the technique aloud.
- Describe how the author uses the technique or convention.
- Explain a strategy students can use to try out the technique or convention.

③ Try it
(1–3 minutes)
Students have a go with what you just taught.

④ Link
(1 minute)
Set an expectation that many students will try what you taught in their writing today.

⬇ **Online Resource 7.1**
Table Tent: Mini-Lesson (Direct Instruction)

→ The share screen and annotation functions on your video conferencing platform will enable you to make the mentor text visible and highlight the part(s) you're discussing.

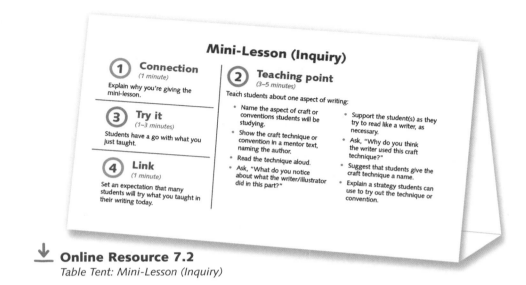

Mini-Lesson (Inquiry)

① Connection
(1 minute)

Explain why you're giving the mini-lesson.

③ Try it
(1–3 minutes)

Students have a go with what you just taught.

④ Link
(1 minute)

Set an expectation that many students will try what you taught in their writing today.

② Teaching point
(3–5 minutes)

Teach students about one aspect of writing:

- Name the aspect of craft or conventions students will be studying.
- Show the craft technique or convention in a mentor text, naming the author.
- Read the technique aloud.
- Ask, "What do you notice about what the writer/illustrator did in this part?"

- Support the student(s) as they try to read like a writer, as necessary.
- Ask, "Why do you think the writer used this craft technique?"
- Suggest that students give the craft technique a name.
- Explain a strategy students can use to try out the technique or convention.

⬇ **Online Resource 7.2**
Table Tent: Mini-Lesson (Inquiry)

→ For more information about teaching mini-lessons, see Lisa Eickholdt and Patty Vitale's *A Teacher's Guide to Writing Workshop Minilessons* (2022).

Small-Group Lessons

After the mini-lesson, students work on their writing independently for 25–30 minutes. Although you'll spend most of this time having one-on-one writing conferences with students, you'll also teach small-group lessons for 3–5 students (Serravallo 2021). Like mini-lessons, many small-group lessons will be about craft techniques or conventions.

▷ **Video 7.5**

▷ **Video 7.6**

Small-group lesson—primary grades

Small-group lesson—upper grades

You'll teach small-group lessons for several reasons:

You have a large class, and you can't get to enough students each week if you only have writing conferences.

Several students were absent for an important mini-lesson or need to hear it again in a more differentiated way.

You see that several students have a similar issue as writers.

You want to give enrichment lessons you aren't going to teach to the whole class in the current unit of study.

Some students need some extra support.

Small-Group Lesson (Direct Instruction)

① Connection
(1 minute)

Explain why you're giving the small-group lesson.

② Teaching point
(3–5 minutes)

Teach students about one aspect of writing:

- Name what you're teaching.
- Explain its importance.
- Show the craft technique or convention in a mentor text, naming the author.

- Read the technique aloud.
- Describe how the author uses the technique or convention.
- Explain a strategy students can use to try out the technique or convention.

③ Try it
(1–3 minutes)

Coach each student individually as they have a go with what you taught.

④ Link
(1 minute)

Set an expectation the students will continue to try what you taught in their writing.

 Online Resource 7.3
Table Tent: Small-Group Lesson (Direct Instruction)

Lesson Prep: SMALL GROUPS

The preparation for small-group lessons is similar to preparing for a mini-lesson. However, if you plan on sitting at a table with students without the ability to project the text, give students a copy of the text or an excerpt of it. If you're teaching online, the preparation for small groups is the same as for mini-lessons.

→ You might meet with a small group as part of a meeting scheduled just for these students, or you might meet them in a breakout room if your entire class is present for a synchronous writing workshop.

→ Just as in a mini-lesson, the share screen and annotation functions on your online platform are important tools.

→ For more information about teaching small-group lessons, see Jennifer Serravallo's *Teaching Writing in Small Groups* (2021).

Small-group lessons have the same structure as mini-lessons. Within that structure, there are a few similarities and differences you'll want to keep in mind:

> When you're teaching a mini-lesson, you're teaching in response to needs that many, but not all, students may have as writers. In a small group, every child has a similar need. Make this clear in the connection, and you may find that students buy into your teaching more because they know it addresses each of them directly.

> As in mini-lessons, you'll teach craft techniques through direct instruction or inquiry, making the same teaching moves.

> During the try-it part of the small-group lesson, you'll check in with and coach each student as they try what you taught.

Small-Group Lesson (Inquiry)

① Connection
(1 minute)

Explain why you're giving the small-group lesson.

② Teaching point
(3–5 minutes)

Teach students about one aspect of writing:

- Name the aspect of craft or conventions students will be studying.
- Show the craft technique or convention in a mentor text, naming the author.
- Read the technique aloud.
- Ask, "What do you notice about what the writer/illustrator did in this part?"

- Support the student(s) as they try to read like a writer, as necessary.
- Ask, "Why do you think the writer used this craft technique?"
- Suggest that students give the craft technique a name.
- Explain a strategy students can use to try out the technique or convention.

③ Try it
(1–3 minutes)

Coach each student individually as they have a go with what you taught.

④ Link
(1 minute)

Set an expectation the students will continue to try what you taught in their writing.

 Online Resource 7.4
Table Tent: Small-Group Lesson (Inquiry)

A Teacher's Guide to Mentor Texts

Writing Conferences

The most important teaching you do in writing workshop happens in your writing conferences. This is because in these one-on-one conversations with students, you're best able to differentiate instruction and meet your students' varied needs as writers.

How Does a Craft or Conventions Conference Go?

When you confer, you have to be ready to think on your feet. First, you figure out what the focus of the conference should be, and then, if you're going to have a craft or convention conference, you decide what to teach the student, select which mentor text to use, and then teach, all in the several minutes that conferences usually take.

This thinking and decision-making happens across the three parts of a writing conference:

In the first part of a conference, you discover what kind of work a student is doing as a writer.	**In the second part of a conference, you assess how well a child is doing the work they're doing and decide what to teach them.**	**In the third part of a conference, you teach the student how to do the work they're doing better.**

Conference Tips

> **Confer where students sit in the classroom or at a special conferring table.**

> **Sit next to the student, as close to eye level as possible.**

> **The tone of conferences should be friendly, warm, and inviting.**

> **Conferences are conversations, and there should be a give-and-take between you and the student.**

> **Conferences are usually 5–7 minutes long.**

> **Try to see 3–5 students during independent writing each day, unless you're teaching a small group, which means you'll have time to confer with 2 or 3 students.**

> **Keep notes about which students you see, and the date you see them, as well as what you learn about and teach each student.**

> **The goal of a conference is to teach students *one* thing that will help them be better writers—in a craft conference, *one* crafting move, or in a conventions conference, *one* convention.**

> **For more information about writing conferences, read my books, *A Teacher's Guide to Writing Conferences* (which contains numerous videos of conferences in which I teach craft techniques and conventions using mentor texts) and *How's It Going? A Practical Guide to Conferring with Student Writers* (2000). Dan Feigelson's book *Radical Listening* (2022) is another conferring resource.**

Part 1: Discover what kind of work a student is doing as a writer.

To figure out what the focus of a conference is going to be, begin by asking students an open-ended question, such as "How's it going?" or "What are you doing as a writer today?" and then give them some wait time so that they can think about how to respond. Optimally, students will tell you what they're doing as writers (Anderson 2000; 2018).

Usually, you'll know the focus of a conference is going to be craft or conventions because students will tell you they're doing one of these kinds of work!

▷ **Videos 7.7–7.13**

Writing Conferences—primary grades

▷ **Videos 7.14–7.19**

Writing Conferences—upper grades

What does the beginning of a craft conference sound like?

Beginning of a Craft Conference

Teacher: How's it going?

Student: I'd like to write a different ending to my memoir.

Teacher: Say more about that . . .

Student: It seems kind of ordinary. I'd like it to be more interesting, like the endings we've talked about.

What does the beginning of a conventions conference sound like?

Beginning of a Conventions Conference

Teacher: What are you doing as a writer today?

Student: I've been putting uppercase letters at the beginning of my sentences, like I did here *(points to the beginning of a sentence in his book).*

Teacher: So you do some editing when you're almost finished with a piece, and you pay attention to capitalization. Anything else you think about?

Student: Usually, I like to make sure periods go at the end of my sentences, but that's a little hard for me.

Online Teaching Tip

→ Read my article, "10 Tips for Conferring with Student Writers Online," for information about how to conduct writing conferences with students on online platforms (Online Resource 7.7, p. 120). The article contains tips for how to teach with mentor texts online and more.

As part of the conversation in the beginning moments of a conference, you can also directly ask students about the craft or conventions work they're doing by asking one or more of these questions:

What are you doing to write well?	What craft moves are you trying? Which one(s) would you like to try?	What are you doing as a writer that you've seen in one of our mentor texts?
	What conventions are you working on?	What conventions have you seen authors use in mentor texts that you're trying to use yourself? Or you would like to use?

In some conferences, students don't say that much about what they're doing as writers when you ask, "How's it going?" Try one of these strategies to get the conversation going:

Ask students if they're having any problems you can help them with.	Ask students to look at their writing and describe what they're doing as a writer in their drafts.	Show students a chart of recent mini-lessons, and ask them which one(s) they're trying.

Ultimately, if students don't tell you what they're doing, look at their writing and try to figure out what they're doing as writers. See if students could try a recent mini-lesson or if they're trying a recent mini-lesson they need some help with. Also look for whether they're working on something that you've talked about in previous conferences that they could still use some help with.

Part 2: Assess the work the student is doing, and decide what to teach.

Once you know what kind of craft or convention conference you're going to have with students, your next step is to decide what to teach them.

1
Read their writing and ask yourself, "What does this student know so far about doing this kind of craft or conventions work?" That is, you'll look for the *partial understanding* the student has of the work.

2
To decide what to teach, ask yourself, "Considering what the child knows so far, what is a next step for them?"

3
Finally, ask yourself, "Which mentor text in my stack shows this next step?"

Part 3: Teach the student how to do what they're doing better.

In the third part of a conference, you'll make four moves:

1
First, you'll give students *feedback* by naming what they understand so far about the work they're doing and the next step they need to take.

2
Then, you'll *teach*. In craft and conventions conferences, this is where you'll show students mentor texts and you'll teach by direct instruction or inquiry.

3
Next, you'll coach the student as they *have a go* with what you taught.

4
Finally, you'll *link* the conference to the student's independent work.

Lesson Prep:
WRITING CONFERENCES

Unlike mini-lessons and small groups, where you know what you're teaching beforehand and have already selected which mentor text you're going to use in the lesson, when you begin a conference, you don't know exactly what you'll teach students—and which mentor text you'll use. This means you'll need to prepare differently for conferences, so you're ready to teach one of a wide variety of craft techniques or conventions.

You'll prepare for conferences by having your stack of mentor texts for the current unit with you when you confer. Usually, a stack contains three or four different texts. You won't need more than that because each of the texts in the stack will enable you to teach many different craft techniques and conventions.

Which texts go in your stack has to do with the kind of unit of study you're doing with your class (next page). When you put together a stack for a unit, include texts that contain examples of the kinds of craft techniques you're studying in the unit. In a genre study, your stack will contain only examples of the genre you're studying with your class, while in other kinds of craft studies, your stack will include a variety of genres. This is because in these other kinds of units, students often write in a variety of genres, and they need to see that craft techniques can be used across genres.

As you get deeper into the year, you'll probably include some texts you used in previous units in your stacks and use them to teach other kinds of craft techniques. When students are already familiar with a text, they can jump right into studying it.

Since the stack in any unit will also contain the conventions you want to teach, you can use the same texts when you have conventions conferences.

Units of Study that Focus on Craft

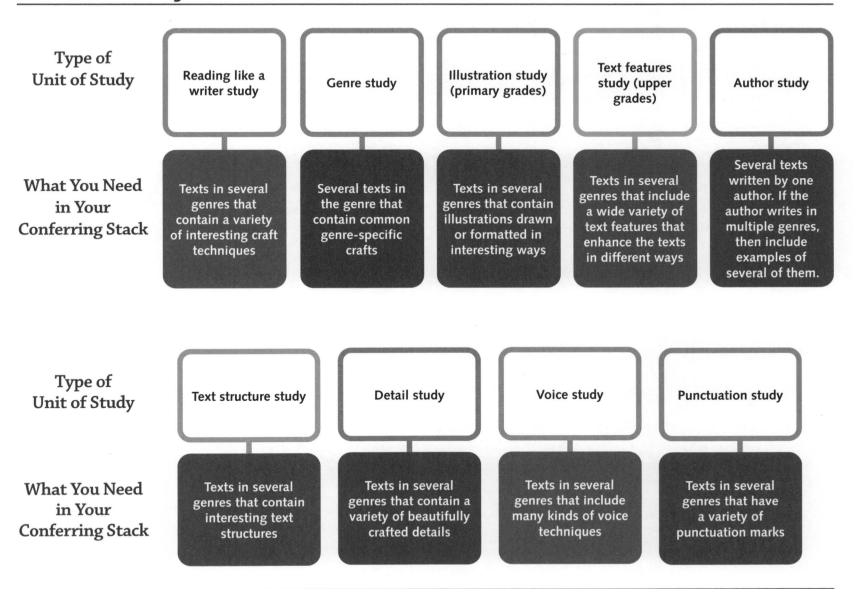

Type of Unit of Study	Reading like a writer study	Genre study	Illustration study (primary grades)	Text features study (upper grades)	Author study
What You Need in Your Conferring Stack	Texts in several genres that contain a variety of interesting craft techniques	Several texts in the genre that contain common genre-specific crafts	Texts in several genres that contain illustrations drawn or formatted in interesting ways	Texts in several genres that include a wide variety of text features that enhance the texts in different ways	Several texts written by one author. If the author writes in multiple genres, then include examples of several of them.

Type of Unit of Study	Text structure study	Detail study	Voice study	Punctuation study
What You Need in Your Conferring Stack	Texts in several genres that contain interesting text structures	Texts in several genres that contain a variety of beautifully crafted details	Texts in several genres that include many kinds of voice techniques	Texts in several genres that have a variety of punctuation marks

Online Resource 7.5

Table Tent: Writing Conference (Direct Instruction)

Online Resource 7.6

Table Tent: Writing Conference (Inquiry)

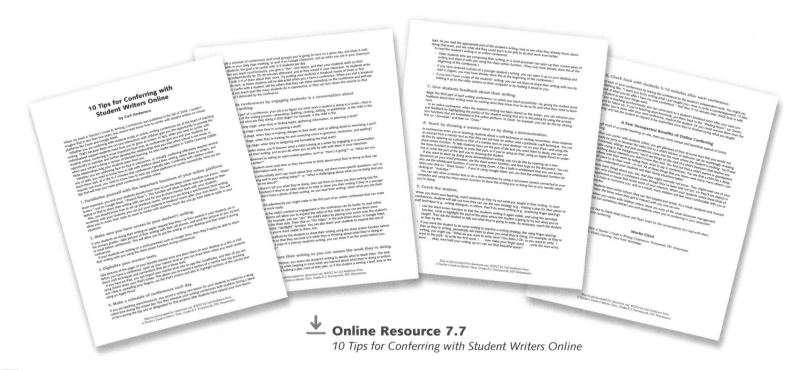

Online Resource 7.7

10 Tips for Conferring with Student Writers Online

A Teacher's Guide to Mentor Texts

Q&A

How do I use share sessions to support students?

The share session that ends writing workshop on most days can be a powerful time for students to discuss the craft and conventions work they did during independent writing that day. Coming together like this helps students feel they are part of a community of writers who are learning together about craft and conventions. And by seeing and hearing what their classmates are doing as writers, students learn about things they can likewise do.

There are several kinds of share sessions. In each, it will make sense for you to refer to the class mentor texts and point out how students are learning from them:

1. **Shares about that day's mini-lesson.** Start some shares by asking students who tried that day's mini-lesson. If you used a mentor text to teach about a craft technique or convention, ask several students to show how they incorporated what they learned from the text in their writing. You might say, "Who tried out what we learned from Jacqueline Woodson in the mini-lesson today?" Students who volunteer to share might read their writing aloud to the class and might

even use the document camera to show the class their writing at the same time, if one is available. As they do so, ask them to name what they did that they learned from the mentor author. And if you see something they did that they don't name, do so yourself. Or, instead of asking students to volunteer, ask students who you conferred with that period about the mini-lesson to share their work.

2. **Shares about interesting things students tried as writers that day.** You can start other shares by asking students who tried something interesting as a writer that period. To get students to talk explicitly about how they're trying out new craft moves, you might ask, "Who tried something today they learned from one of our class mentor texts?" Sometimes students will share craft moves or conventions they learned from your lessons or from whole-class craft study—and sometimes they'll share things they've noticed on their own!

☆Tip

→ Help students learn from their own mentor texts!

As the year progresses, you can invite students to find and study their own mentor texts. Students might find mentor texts in your classroom library, at home, or online. Sometimes a text a student finds can even become a class mentor text!

When students have their own mentor texts, writing conferences are the best time to give them support in learning from them. In the beginning of conferences, ask students "What have you noticed in your mentor text that you want to try yourself?" and have them show you the crafting move or con-vention they want to try. Then give them the support they need to be successful with it.

Since students will need to find their own mentor texts in the future when they write, inviting them to do this in your class will give them practice with this skill.

Q & A ✳

What do I do when students . . .

✳ **Notice craft moves in mentor texts, but aren't yet trying them in their writing?**

In mini-lessons and small groups, model how you try out craft techniques. Also, in conferences, give students one-on-one support with trying out crafting moves.

✳ **Use a craft technique exactly like a mentor author?**

Students commonly respond to craft instruction by doing literally what mentor authors do—for example, they include the same number of reasons they see the mentor author use, or they'll write the same number of lines of dialogue. One way you can help students generalize what a mentor author does is to show them how other authors use the same technique, but slightly differently—you could show an opinion mentor with a different number of reasons, or a narrative with dialogue that goes back and forth a different number of times.

✳ **Try a craft move just once that could be used across a text?**

Show students how mentor authors use this move multiple times in a text, and explain why. Also, model in your own writing how you use the craft technique across a text.

✳ **Don't continue to use craft techniques you study in one unit in subsequent ones.**

Keep up the charts of craft techniques you've studied with your class in one unit during later units, and remind students they can continue to use them. You can also give students a copy of these charts to keep in their folders for reference.

✳ **Overuse a craft technique?**

Look at mentor texts with students and study how often the authors actually use the craft technique.

Try It Yourself: Improve Your Teaching

With these exercises, you can practice the different teaching moves. Ultimately, you'll gain skill by practicing these moves over and over, until they become part of your conferring repertoire.

1 Read a piece of student writing and identify a craft technique or convention you could teach the student. Then write out a transcript of a direct instruction lesson you could have with the child. Then reread the section of this chapter on direct instruction, and use it to make revisions to what you wrote. By doing this exercise once—or several times— you'll get better at doing this kind of lesson, and you'll be able to step into an actual mini-lesson, small group, or writing conference with more confidence.

2 Do the same, but this time write an inquiry lesson.

3 Use your smartphone or iPad to videotape a few of your mini-lessons, small groups, and conferences with students. Later, watch them and assess which teaching moves you made successfully and which moves still need work.

4 Ask a fellow teacher, coach, or principal who has read this chapter to visit your classroom and watch you do craft and conventions lessons. Afterward, ask the observer to give you feedback about the moves you made and make suggestions about how to improve your teaching.

References

Als, Hilton. 2003. "Tony Morrison and the Ghosts in the House." *The New Yorker*, October 20.

Anderson, Carl. 2000. *How's It Going? A Practical Guide to Conferring with Student Writers*. Portsmouth, NH: Heinemann.

_____. 2005. *Assessing Writers*. Portsmouth, NH: Heinemann.

_____. 2018. *A Teacher's Guide to Writing Conferences*. Portsmouth, NH: Heinemann.

Bishop, Rudine Sims. 1990. "Mirrors, Windows and Sliding Glass Doors." *Perspectives*, 1(3), pp ix – xi.

Bomer, Katherine. 2005. *Writing a Life*. Portsmouth, NH: Heinemann.

_____. 2016. *The Journey Is Everything*. Portsmouth, NH: Heinemann.

Bomer, Katherine and Corrine Arens. 2020. *A Teacher's Guide to Writing Workshop Essentials: Time, Choice, Response*. Portsmouth, NH: Heinemann.

Bomer, Katherine and Corrine Arens. 2020. A *Teacher's Guide to Writing Workshop Essentials: Time, Choice, Response*. Portsmouth, NH: Heinemann.

Caine, Karen. 2008. *Writing to Persuade*. Portsmouth, NH: Heinemann.

Calkins, Lucy. 1994. *The Art of Teaching Writing*. Portsmouth, NH: Heinemann.

Calkins, Lucy, and colleagues. 2013. *Units of Study in Opinion, Information, and Narrative Writing, Elementary Series Bundle, Grades K–5*. Portsmouth, NH: Heinemann.

Canfield, Jack, M. V. Hanson, and P. Hanson. 2021. *Chicken Soup for the Preteen Soul: 21st Anniversary Edition*. New York: Simon and Shuster.

Chase, Carole F., ed. 2001. *Madeleine L'Engle Herself: Reflections on a Writing Life*. New York: Convergent.

Chavez, Felicia Rose. 2021. *The Anti-Racist Writing Workshop: How to Decolonize the Creative Classroom*. Chicago: Haymarket Books.

Cleary, Beverly. *Ramona Quimby, Age 8*. New York: Harper Collins.

Cornwall, Gaia. 2017. *Jabari Jumps*. Somerville, MA: Candlewick.

Cruz, M. Colleen. 2018. *Writers Read Better: Nonfiction*. Thousand Oaks, CA: Corwin.

_____. 2019. *Writers Read Better: Narrative*. Thousand Oaks, CA: Corwin.

Education Northwest. 2020. "What Are the Traits?" https://educationnorthwest.org/traits

Ebarvia, Tricia. 2017. "Tricia Ebarvia: How Inclusive Is Your Literacy Classroom Really?" Heinemann Blog, December 12. https://blog.heinemann.com/heinemann-fellow-tricia-ebavaria-inclusive-literacy-classroom-really.

Eickholdt, Lisa, and Patty Vitale-Reilly. 2022. *A Teacher's Guide to Writing Workshop Minilessons*. Portsmouth, NH: Heinemann.

Feigelson, Dan. 2009. *Practical Punctuation: Lessons of Rule Making and Rule Breaking in Elementary Writing*. Portsmouth, NH: Heinemann.

_____. 2022. *Radical Listening: Reading and Writing Conferences to Reach All Students*. New York: Scholastic.

Fletcher, Ralph. 2012. *Marshfield Dreams: When I Was a Kid*. New York: Square Fish.

_____. 2013. *What a Writer Needs*. 2nd ed. Portsmouth, NH: Heinemann.

_____. 2015. *Making Nonfiction from Scratch*. Portland, ME: Stenhouse.

_____. 2019. *Focus Lessons*. Portsmouth, NH: Heinemann.

_____. (@FletcherRalph). 2022. "What do we mean by . . ." Twitter, February 18, 8:19 a.m. https://twitter.com/FletcherRalph/status/1494662781919969283?cxt=HHwWhoCy9bH4jb4pAAAA.

Fletcher, Ralph, and JoAnn Portalupi. 2001a. *Nonfiction Craft Lessons: Teaching Information Writing K–8*. Portland, ME: Stenhouse.

_____. 2001b. *Writing Workshop: The Essential Guide*. Portsmouth, NH: Heinemann.

_____. 2007. *Craft Lessons: Teaching Writing K–8*. Portland, ME: Stenhouse.

Fox, Mem. 1993. *Radical Reflections: Passionate Opinions on Teaching, Learning, and Living*. New York: Harvest.

Glover, Matt. 2019. *Craft and Process Studies*. Portsmouth, NH: Heinemann.

Glover, Matt, and Mary Alice Berry. 2012. *Projecting Possibilities for Writers: The How, What & Why of Designing Units of Study*. Portsmouth, NH: Heinemann.

Hartsell, Mark. 2011. "'Reading Is Not Optional': Walter Dean Myers Becomes Third National Ambassador for Young People's Literature." Newsletter, Center for the Book in the Library of Congress. https://guides.loc.gov /youth-ambassador-walter-dean-myers/reading-is-not-optional.

Hattie, John. 2009. *Visible Learning*. New York: Routledge.

Heard, Georgia. 1989. *For the Good of the Earth and Sun: Teaching Poetry*. Portsmouth, NH: Heinemann.

———. 1999. *Awakening the Heart*. Portsmouth, NH: Heinemann.

———. 2013. *Finding the Heart of Nonfiction*. Portsmouth, NH: Heinemann.

Huyck, Liz. 2019. "Surprising Saturn." *Ask* 18(8): pp. 6–11.

Jackson, Peter, dir. 2021. *The Beatles: Get Back*. Apple Corps, Ltd., Walt Disney Studios, and Wingnut Films.

Kalish, Nancy. 2009. "Summer Homework Should Be Banned." *Time for Kids:2009*.

Keene, Ellin Oliver. 2022. *The Literacy Studio: Redesigning the Workshop for Readers and Writer*. Portsmouth, NH: Heinemann.

King, Stephen. 2000. *On Writing: A Memoir of the Craft*. New York: Simon & Schuster.

Klein, Christopher. 2020. "The Remarkable Story of Maya Lin's Vietnam Veterans Memorial." Biography.com. https://www.biography.com /news/maya-lin-vietnam-veterans-memorial.

Laminack, Lester. 2016. *Cracking Open the Author's Craft*. New York: Scholastic.

Lane, Barry. 2015. *After the End*. 2nd ed. Portsmouth, NH: Heinemann.

Lehman, Christopher. 2012. *Energize Research Reading and Writing*. Portsmouth, NH: Heinemann.

Linder, Rozlyn. 2016. *The Big Book of Details*. Portsmouth, NH: Heinemann.

Marchetti, Allison, and Rebekah O'Dell. 2015. *Writing with Mentors*. Portsmouth, NH: Heinemann.

Medina, Meg. 2020. *Evelyn Del Rey Is Moving Away*. Somerville, MA: Candlewick.

Meyers, Christopher. 2014. "The Apartheid of Children's Literature." *New York Times*, March 15.

Muhammad, Ibtihaj. 2019. *The Proudest Blue: A Story of Hijab and Family*. New York Little, Brown and Company.

Newkirk, Tom (@Tom_Newkirk). 2021. "Students need to read . . ." Twitter, December 5, 2021, 10:10 a.m. https://twitter.com/Tom_Newkirk /status/1467511822270046210.

Panagiotakopoulos, Foti. 2019. "The Origin of 'Mentor' Comes Straight Out of Greek Mythology (And the Story's Epic!)." January 24. https://www. growthmentor.com/blog/origin-of-word-mentor/.

Park, Eleanor. 2020. "Maya Lin: The Influence of Asian-American Heritage on Artistic Identity. The Diversity Story. July 10. https://www .thediversitystory.org/post/maya-lin-the-influence-of-asian -american-heritage-on-artistic-identity.

Pullman, Phillip (@PhillipPullman). n.d. Twitter bio. https://twitter.com /PhilipPullman?ref_src=twsrc%5Egoogle%7Ctwcamp%5Eser- p%7Ctwgr%5Eauthor.

Ray, Katie Wood. 1999. *Wondrous Words*. Urbana, IL: NCTE.

———. 2002. *What You Know by Heart: How to Develop Curriculum for Your Writing Workshop*. Portsmouth, NH: Heinemann.

———. 2006. *Study Driven: A Framework for Planning Units of Study in the Writing Workshop*. Portsmouth, NH: Heinemann.

———. 2010. *In Pictures and Words*. Portsmouth, NH: Heinemann.

Reynolds, Jason. 2019. *Look Both Ways*. New York: Atheneum/Caitlyn Dlouhy Books.

Rodman, Mary Ann. 2005. *My Best Friend*. New York: Penguin Group.

Rylant, Cynthia. 1996. *The Whales*. New York: Blue Sky Press.

Salesses, Matthew. 2021. *Craft in the Real World: Rethinking Fiction Writing and Workshopping*. New York: Catapult.

Schreiber, Anne. 2008. *Sharks*. Washington, D.C.: National Geographic Society.

Serravallo, Jennifer. 2017. *The Writing Strategies Book*. Portsmouth, NH: Heinemann.

————. 2021. *Teaching Writing in Small Groups*. Portsmouth, NH: Heinemann.

Shubitz, Stacey. 2016. *Craft Moves*. Portland, ME: Stenhouse.

Shubitz, Stacey and Lynne R. Dorfman. 2019. *Welcome to Writing Workshop: Engaging Today's Students with A Model that Works*. Portland, ME: Stenhouse.

Smith, Frank. 1983. "Reading Like a Writer." *Language Arts* 26(5): 558–67.

————. 1988. *Joining the Literacy Club*. Portsmouth, NH: Heinemann.

Stewart, Melissa. 2011. *Deadliest Animals*. Washington, D.C.: National Geographic Society.

Stewart, Melissa, and Marlene Correia. 2021. *5 Kinds of Nonfiction: Enriching Reading and Writing Instruction with Children's Books*. Portland, ME: Stenhouse.

Sundem, Garth. 2010. *Real Kids, Real Stories, Real Change*. Minneapolis, MN: Free Spirit Publishing.

VanDerwater, Amy. 2018. *Poems Are Teachers: How Studying Writing Strengthens Writing in All Genres*. Portsmouth, NH: Heinemann.

Walther, Maria and Karen Biggs-Tucker. 2020. *The Literacy Workshop: Where Reading and Writing Converge*. Portland, ME: Stenhouse.

The Whitney Museum. Exhibition. "Vida Americana: Mexican Muralists Remake American Art." February 17, 2020–January 31, 2021.

Woodson, Jacqueline. 2015. "Jacqueline Woodson on Growing Up, Coming Out and Saying Hi to Strangers." Interview by David Bianculli. *Fresh Air*. NPR. June 19. https://www.npr.org/2015/06/19 /415747871/jacqueline-woodson-on-growing-up-coming-out -and-saying-hi-to-strangers.

————. 2016. *Brown Girl Dreaming*. New York: Puffin Books.